Software Testing and QTP Automation

Rajamanickam Antonimuthu

ISBN: 1484039556
ISBN-13: 978-1484039557

Contents

Importance of Software Testing..5
Basics of Quality Assurance (QA) in Software Development........7
Software Testing Terms 8
Writing Good Test Cases and Finding Bugs effectively..............19
Tips and Tricks for doing AdHoc Testing...................................22
Best practices in Software Testing..24
Importance of Software Test Automation using tools such as QTP
....27
Need of Domain Knowledge for Software Testers 29
Software Test Automation tool evaluation 30
The need for having development/programming knowledge for
Software Testers..33
Software Testing Questions and Answers 34
Answers 46
Introduction to QTP..47
How to Learn QTP? 51
Understanding Object Repository..55
Different Types of Object Repositories 60
Local Object Repository 60
Shared Object Repository 61
Associating Repositories 61
Understanding Action Iteration and Test Iteration.....................62
Recording Modes...65
Run Modes 66
CheckPoints...67
Data Tables..68
QTP Result Window..69
Recovery Scenario..70
Synchronization 71
Automation Object Model 72
Handling Passwords in QTP Scripts 72
Required Steps/Processes in QTP Automation............................75

Best Practices in QTP Automation 79
Scheduling QTP Script Execution 80
Basics of vbscript 84
KeyWord Driven Testing and Framework in QTP 91
Descriptive Programming in QTP 94
Managing Object Repositories in QTP 96
Object Spy in QTP 100
QTP methods and script for reading object properties 102
Tips for doing effective QTP script Development 105
Some Thoughts on QTP Interview 106
QTP trial version installation 114
Wish list for the QTP future release. 114
QTP Questions and Answers 116

Importance of Software Testing

It will be good to know the reasons for learning software testing before start learning it. In Internet, we can see lot of articles explaining/listing loss made by poor low-quality software products.

How will you feel if a **bug** in bank software shows your bank **balance as 0** instead of some thousands?
And if you are a student, what will be your state if your mark-sheet shows your **score as 0** instead of some good score?

Here, we will be feeling good if we see some notification or message instead of seeing **wrong data.**

For example, a message such as *"Not able to show your balance due to some unexpected error* "will do more goodness than showing balance as 0 in our first example.

Similarly, a message such as *"Couldn't print your mark-sheet because of unexpected issue"* will be useful than showing score as 0 in our second example.

Testing plays an important role to avoid these situations.

So, we can say that testing is necessary or important even when it couldn't guarantee **100% error free** software application.

i-e Testing may not fix the issues, but definitely will help to provide improved user-friendliness.

Also,

- Cost of fixing the bug will be more if it is found in later stage than it is **found earlier**.
- Quality can be ensured by testing only. In the competitive market, **only Quality product can exist for long time.**

Testing will be necessary even if it is not possible to do **100% testing** for an application.

One more important reason for doing testing is user/production environment will be completely **different from development environment.**

For example, a webpage developer may be using FireFox as browser for doing his webpage development. But the user may be using different browser such as Internet Explorer, Safari, Chrome and Opera.

The web page which is appearing good in FireFox may not appear good in other browsers (particularly IE). So ultimately, user will not be happy even if the developer puts more efforts to develop the webpage. **User's** satisfaction is more important for growth of any business, so testing becomes more important.

And, we can assume/treat the **Testers as the representatives of the Users**.

These days Software Development and Web development are becoming more complex. So, writing bug-free code becomes extremely difficult, even for highly experienced programmers.

But our reliance on software for performing everyday tasks in the medical, telecommunications, manufacturing, and financial industries is getting increased day by day.

So, the need for a system to deliver a bug free Software is increased. Quality software can't be created with an ad- hoc, part-time, bug hunt. It requires a methodical and disciplined approach to preventing, finding, and reporting bugs. Software Testing will show you what it takes to be a successful software tester, assuring that you discover those nasty bugs before your customers do.

Basics of Quality Assurance (QA) in Software Development

I believe the previous chapter explained the importance or need for the Software testing. In this chapter we can see some basics of Software Testing or Quality Assurance.

Quality Assurance is the most important factor in any business or industry.
Same thing is applicable for **Software development** also.
Spending some additional money for getting high quality product will definitely give more **profit**.

But, it is not true that expensive products are high-quality products. Even an inexpensive or cheap product can be high-quality product if it meets Customer's needs/expectation.

The quality assurance cycle consists of four steps: *Plan, Do, Check,* and *Act.* These steps are commonly abbreviated as **PDCA**.

The four quality assurance steps within the PDCA model are

- **Plan:** Establish objectives and processes required to deliver the desired results.
- **Do:** Implement the process developed.

- **Check:** Monitor and evaluate the implemented process by testing the results against the predetermined objectives
- **Act:** Apply actions necessary for improvement if the results require changes.

For getting appropriate quality output in software development we need to follow **SQA (Software Quality Assurance)** process in each phase (*Planning, Requirement Analysis, Design, Development, Integration & Test, Implementation and Maintenance*) of the software development lifecycle.

We should follow below solutions to avoid many software development problems.

- **Solid requirements** - Clear, complete, attainable, detailed and testable requirements that are agreed by all players (Customer, developers and Testers).
- **Realistic schedules** - Allocate enough time for planning, design, testing, bug fixing, re-testing and documentation.
- **Adequate testing** - Start testing early, re-test after fixes/changes.
- **Avoid unnecessary changes** in initial requirements once after starting the coding.
- Require **walk-through** and inspections.

Software Testing Terms

In previous chapters we have learned about importance and some basics of software Testing.

Now we can go in detail about software Testing.

Before going in detail, it is better to have clear understanding of Terms used in Software Testing.

Find below the meaning/definition of Terms frequently used in Software Testing. Note that I am defining these terms using my own words to explain it easily. It may not be the exact definition. You can refer any **ISTQB** documentation if you want to know the exact definition.

Software Development Life Cycle (SDLC)

SDLC involves different phases such as Initial/Planning phase, Requirement analysis phase, Design phase, Coding phase, Testing phase, Delivery and Maintenance phase.

All these phases can be followed one by one linearly as **Waterfall model** or they can be followed as **V-model** which expects doing testing activities in parallel with development activities.

Initial Phase involves gathering requirements by interacting with the Customer. Normally Business Analyst will do this and will prepare a requirement document.

Here Customer is the internal marketing team in case of **product** development. Otherwise Customer is the person who is paying for doing the **project.**

Requirement analysis phase involves doing detailed study of the customer requirements and judging possibilities and scope of the requirements. And it involves tentative planning and technology & resource selection.

SRS (System Requirement Specification) will be created in this phase.

Design phase involves dividing the whole project into modules and sub-modules by doing High level Designing (H.L.D) and   Low level Designing   (L.L.D).

Coding Phase involves creating source code or program by the programmers by referring the design document. Coding standards with proper comments should be followed.

Testing Phase involves getting clarification for the unclear requirements and then writing test cases by Testing Team based on the requirements. And, the testing team will execute the test cases once the build is released and they will report the bugs found during the test case execution.

Delivery & Maintenance phase involves installing the application in the customer place and providing the details such as release notes to the customer.

Maintenance or support Team will help the customers if they face any issue when using the application.

Software Testing - It is the process of verifying whether a software application or a software product **meets** the **business and technical requirements**. i-e verifying whether the developed software application works **as expected**.

It will be done by comparing the Actual result against the Expected Result.

For example, if the requirement says *"After entering valid username and password the user should be logged in to the website"* software testing is nothing but just entering valid username and password to verify whether the user got logged in to the website.

But, doing software testing is not so simple, lot of complex factors involved in doing testing. It needs lot of thinking and brainstorming processes.

In this simple example, we should know below things.

→ In which **environment** we need to do the login testing?

→ What is **valid** username and password? i-e *Minimum and Maximum length of username and what are the allowed special characters.*

→ How to verify whether the user **really logged** into the website?

→ **How long** it will take to complete the login?

→ How the system should behave if the user enters **invalid username** or invalid password?

→ What will happen if the user **already logged in**?

→ How the system should behave if someone **continuously try to login** by giving invalid username and password?

→ Is it possible to reach the target page **even without doing login**?

→ How the system will behave if there is any **network issue** once after entering the username and password?

→ What will happen if two people try to login **with same username and password simultaneously** from two different machines?

→ How the system will behave if the user **doesn't use the website for longtime** once after getting logged in?

→ Will the login process take same time even after **Millions of users registered** with the system?

→ What will happen if thousands of people try to do login at **same time**?

→ What **message** will be shown to the user if the database which stores the user details goes down?

→ Will the system provide any other interface (e.g **API, webservice**) other than the standard UI for doing login?

→ How to help the user if he forgot the password? Whether we can store the password in **plain text** format and send it to the email id of the user? Or store the password in **encrypted** format and reset it to a randomly generated password and send it to the email id of the user?

→ Will the system allow the username in **non-English** also?

→ Most importantly, when we need to do this login testing?

→ What are the **pre-requisites**? (e.g user should be registered before testing login).

→ Is it necessary to do the testing in **production environment** also?

→ To whom should we report if the Testing fails? And, what are the details we need to provide? How we come to know once it got fixed? What we need to do once after it got fixed?

→ Is there any option (e.g *Remember Me cookie, auto-complete*) for making the login easy? Will these options break the login system in any way?

→ Whether anyone (e.g hacker) can access the password while doing login?

→ Whether the password is not readable to the developers of the system so as to avoid any misuse? (i.e. whether **password encryption is done** before storing it in Database)

→ If we need to do this testing multiple times in many environments, is there any easy way to do the testing? (e.g using scripts and **automation tools** such as QTP)

→ Will it work correctly in different user interfaces (e.g **Different browsers** such as Internet Explorer, FireFox, Safari, Chrome), and in different settings (e.g javascript disabled)?

→ Is the code written well enough so that **future enhancements** can be made easily?

→ Who has to do this testing? Whether the developer of the system can do the testing also?

So, it is important to have **clear understanding** of testing approaches before start doing any testing.

Functional & Non-functional Testing

Functional testing mainly focuses on verifying whether the features requested in the requirement document are working correctly.

Non-functional testing is checking the **performance, stability, scalability, usability, internationalization** and **security** of the software application.

Testing methods

Whitebox, Blackbox and Greybox are three Testing methods.

White box testing will be done by going thro' the coding and by understanding the algorithm used in the coding. It includes API testing and code coverage.

Black box testing will be done without knowing internal structure or coding of the application. It will help to find more bugs effectively. But the tester may spend more time by writing many test cases to check something which could have been tested easily by writing one test case.

Grey box testing involves having knowledge of internal data structures and algorithms for writing the test cases, but testing at the user, or black-box level

Testing levels

Unit Testing or component testing will be done by the developers to make sure that the small piece of the code works correctly.

Each and every unit of the program will be tested in order to confirm whether the conditions, functions and loops are working fine or not.

Integration Testing will help to expose defects in the interfaces and interaction between many different modules of the program.

System testing will be done by the Testing Team to make sure that the program or application meets the requirements.

It includes GUI software testing, Usability testing, Performance testing, Stress testing, Security testing, Scalability testing, Sanity Testing, Smoke Testing, ad hoc testing, etc..

Regression testing will done to make sure that the application or program is not affected by any code change done to the application. i-e Already working functions in other modules of the program should continue to work after changing any of the module .

We need to test each part of application even when the code change is done in any specific part or module of the program. Automation tools will be useful for doing regression testing.

Alpha Testing will be a part of user Acceptance testing. It will be done in the developers premise, and will be done by the customers or by independent test team.

Beta testing comes after alpha testing. Beta versions of the Software will be released to a limited number of people outside of the programming team.

Actual release will be done if there are no major issues found in Beta testing.

Testing Artifacts

Test plan is a document which describes the objectives, scope, approach, and focus of a software testing effort. It will be made available for development team and business people also so that they can understand the testing activities done by Testing Team.

It will cover the features to be tested and features not be tested.

Testing environment details, risks, Responsibilities, testing schedule, Test deliverables and resource allocation details will be included in the Test plan.

So, it will be useful to have overall view of the testing activities to be done in particular release of a software application.

Traceability matrix is simply a mapping between the requirements and the Test cases. It will be prepared in a tabular form. i-e in excel spread sheet.

Once column will have the list of the Requirement IDs and the next column which have Test case IDs which test that requirement.

It will help to make sure that test cases are written well enough to cover all the requirements.

Similarly we can have reverse Traceability matrix also. i-e mapping between test cases and the requirements.

It will help to make sure that we are not having any test cases for the requirements which are not asked by the customer.

Test suite will be the collection of the Test cases. Mostly all relevant test cases will be grouped as one test case document. For example, the test cases which will test the login module will be stored in a particular spread sheet file named as "login_testcases.xls". It can contain information such as Name of the module, description, total number of test cases and details of reference document (i-e requirement document, use case, etc).

Test case will have below things.

Test case ID for uniquely identifying the test case. For example, Test case ID can be TC001,TC002,....

Test case description will have condition which we are going to test.

e.g *To verify user sees the message "invalid login details" when they enter valid username and invalid password"*

Test steps will give details or steps required for executing this test case

e.g 1. Go to the login page

    2. Enter valid username.

    3. Enter invalid password.

    4. Click "login" button.

Expected Result will give the details about the behavior or result we should see once after executing the test steps.

e.g *User should see "invalid login details" message in Red color at top of the page.*

Author who writes this test case.

Automatable- To mark whether this test case can be automated using automation tools such as QTP.

Apart from above things we can add **pass/fail** and **remarks** while executing the test cases.

Test case can be written by referring **use case document and requirement document**. We may need to refer the application for writing test cases.

We can use some techniques such as Equivalence partitioning and boundary value analysis for writing test cases.

According to Equivalence partitioning, writing one test case for each partition of the input data is enough.

For example, if a password field accepts minimum 4 characters and maximum 10 characters, then there will be three partitions. First one is a valid partition 4 to 10. Second is invalid partition of values less than 4. Third one is another invalid partition of values more than 10. We can take one value from each partition to do the testing.

In this example the boundary values based on boundary value analysis are 3,4,5, 9,10 and11.

Software Test life cycle.

Test Planning - Scope of the testing will be defined according to the budget allocated for the testing. And, **Test plan** document will be prepared by the Test manager.

Test development- Test Cases will be written by the Testing Team (QA Team) during this phase. **Test data** files also will be created.

Test execution- Testers will execute the test cases and will report the issues to the development Team for fixing them.

Performance test should be executed only after the functional and regression testing got completed.

Bug Tracking is the methodology used to follow up the bugs/defects/issue found during Test execution. There are many free tools (e.g *Bugzilla.*) available for doing bug tracking effectively.

Normally the bug will be tracked as standard **bug life cycle**.

It will have below states.

New: When a tester finds a bug first time the state will be "NEW". This means that the bug is not yet approved.

Open: After a tester has posted a bug, the lead of the testing team will check whether the reported bug is genuine and the he will change the state as "OPEN".

Assign: The development Team lead will assign the bug to particular developer for fixing it. Now the state will be changed to "ASSIGN".

Ready-to-Test: Once the developer fixes the bug, he will assign the bug to the testing team for next round of testing with the status "READY-TO-TEST".

Deferred: The status will be changed to "DEFERRED" if the team decides to fix it in next release or the priority is very low.

Rejected: If the developer decides that the bug is not genuine, he can reject the bug. Then the state of the bug is changed to "REJECTED".

Duplicate: If the bug is repeated twice or the root causes for two bugs are same, then one bug status will be changed to "DUPLICATE".

Verified: Once the bug is fixed and the status is changed to "Ready-to-test", the tester tests the bug again. If the bug is not present in the software, he approves that the bug is fixed and changes the status to "VERIFIED".

Reopened: If the bug still exists even after the bug is fixed by the developer, the tester will change the status to "REOPENED". The bug will go thro' life cycle once again.

Closed: Once the bug is fixed, it will be tested by the tester again. If the tester verifies that the bug no longer exists in the software, he changes the status of the bug to "CLOSED". This state means that the bug is fixed and tested again.

Reporting- Test summary report should be created for explaining the steps taken for delivering quality product. This summary report should show the number of test cases executed, how many passed and how many failed, test coverage, defect density and other **test metrics**. And, it should show performance test result also.

Writing Good Test Cases and Finding Bugs effectively

To develop bug free software application, writing good test cases is essential.
Here, we will see how to write good test cases. Before seeing this, we should understand what is **Good Test Case**. There won't be any solid definition for *"Good Test Case"*. I will consider a Test Case as **"Good"** only when a Tester feels happy **to follow the steps** in the Test Case which is written by another Tester.

Test Cases will be useful only if they are used by the people.

If a test case is poorly written with **excessive unwanted steps**, then most of the Testers **won't read** it fully. Just they will read few lines and will execute it based on their own understanding which will be **mostly wrong**. On the other hand, if it is having fewer details then it is difficult to execute it. As of now, I am thinking below things for writing effective Test Cases.

- Before start writing test cases, become familiar with the (AUT) Application Under Test. You will become familiar with Application by doing some **adhoc/exploratory testing**.
- We should **read the requirements** clearly and completely. If we have any questions in the Requirements it should be clarified by appropriate person (*e.g Customer or Business Team*). And also, it is good practice to gather some basic domain knowledge before getting into reading requirements and writing Test Cases. And also, we can have discussion/meeting with developers/business team.
- Very Important thing is, we should use only **simple language or style** to write the Test cases so that any one can easily understand without any ambiguity
- Give meaningful and easily understandable **Test case ID/number**.
  For example, if you are writing Test case for testing Login module you can Test Case ID as below.

  1a - for testing positive scenario such as entering valid username and valid password.
  1b - for testing negative scenario such as entering invalid username and invalid password.

  By giving Test Case number as above instead of giving sequential number, we can easily add any new case such as below one without needing to adjust/modify number of any other subsequent test cases.

  1c- for testing negative scenario such as entering valid username and invalid password.

- And also, if we have any similar module we can give separate sequence number for specifying the module.

  For example, assume that we are having separate login modules for User and Admin with little changes.
  In this case we can give number as below,
  1.1-First case in User module.
  1.2-Second case in User module.
  2.1-First case in Admin module

20

2.2-Second case in Admin module.

If Test Description/Steps/Expected Results of 2.1 is mostly same as 1.1 then we should refer 1.1 in 2.1 instead writing the sample details again.

By doing like this, we can avoid redundant details to have clear test case document.

- Test Description should be short and it should uniquely represent the current test scenario without any ambiguity.
- In any situation, **don't use "if condition"** in the Test steps. Always address only one scenario in one test case. It will be helpful to have unambiguous Expected Result.
- Give some sample **test data** that will be useful for executing the test cases.
- If the Test Case requires any **Preconditions/prerequisite** don't forget to mention them.
  The best way is, we should arrange/order the Test Cases such that the need for specifying precondition is minimum.

For example, we need to write test case for testing user creation, user modification and user deletion.

For doing user modification and user deletion we should have already created user as precondition.

If we arrange the Test cases in below mentioned order, we can avoid the need for specifying any preconditions/prerequisites.
1-Test case for creating user.
2-Test case for verifying duplicate/existing user when adding another user with same username.
3-Test case for modifying user.
4-Test case for deleting user.

- Keep **Traceability Matrix** to make sure that we have written test cases for covering all requirements.

- Once after completing all positive scenarios, think about all possibilities of negative scenarios to have test cases which will effectively find most of the bugs.

  For doing this we can refer alternate flow section of use case document, and we can think about different data, boundary conditions, different navigations paths and multi user environment.
- In the test case document, we can give link to screenshots explaining the steps and/or expected results with pictures. But anyway, it is not good practice to place the screenshots within the Test Case document itself unless it is very essential
- Many tools are available to capture the screenshots with user action as video. We can make use of them to keep video explaining the steps and expected results clearly in case the test case requires any complex steps. We can give link to this video from the test case document.

Tips and Tricks for doing AdHoc Testing

It is always not possible to follow proper testing such as writing Test Plan and writing Test cases. In some cases we may need to go with **adHoc Testing** because of time constraint or resource constraint.

AdHoc Testing is the part of **Exploratory** testing. It is done without doing Planning and Documentation. Adhoc testing will help to find the defects earlier. We know that *earlier a defect is found the cheaper it is to fix it.*

Here I am listing some tips for doing adhoc testing effectively.

- In case of UI (User Interface) testing, test all navigation including **Back button** navigation.

  Go thro' all the pages of the application to find any broken links and also make sure that each and every page is having proper links to reach other pages either directly or indirectly.

And, notice the **page loading time** also. If it takes more time then try to narrow down whether it is due to network issue or web server issue or the page issue. i-e If the other domain webpages are loading normally then we can say that it is not due to network issue. And, if other pages in the same domain are loading normally then we can say that it is not related to server issue.

- Check whether all the images are having **alt** attribute. And anchor tags should have title attribute.
- See the application screen or webpage by changing/setting **different screen resolution** in your computer monitor.
- Test the webpage in many **different web browsers** such as Internet Explorer, FireFox, chrome, safari, etc.
- Test the **tab order** and **default focus** in all the pages. Especially study the behaviour of the application when it has more than one submit button.
- Try to enter/save test data having **special characters** such as single quotes, double quotes and comma .
- You can try to enter text with HTML tags such as < and > also in the textbox
- Try to load an authenticated webpage directly by entering URL in the browser without doing login.
- Try all the possibilities of boundary values such as entering lot of data in textbox and entering negative values in numeric fields.
- Remember to navigate the application from two different machines/browsers simultaneously; especially concentrate on to test concurrent database saving/updating operation.
- If possible/necessary, test the application in different OS (Operating System) such as Windows, Linux and MAC.
- If your webpage uses flash files, try to see the behavior of your webpage when it is loaded in a machine which is not having flash player. Normally it should automatically download the flash plug-in.
- Instead of testing everything from your local machine, just try to test some screens by hosting your site in some remote

machine. It will help to identify unexpected issues which may occur due to network latency.

- Test **Session timeout**, Cookie expiry and script execution timeout. For testing these things you should know about session and cookie. Session variables are stored in server side. They will be unique for each browser session. It will expire based on server setting. Cookie will be stored in user browser. It will expire based on the expiry time set while writing the cookie. But the user can manually also delete this cookie from the browser before it actually expires. Since user login status is mostly controlled using session and cookie variables, it is very important to test behavior of the system when the session or cookie expires.

- Try to **refresh** your confirmation screen many times to verify whether the multiple refresh saves/inserts the data multiple times. Normally multiple refresh will insert the data multiple times if the developer forget to handle this scenario.

- Test with different Date and Time format if your webpage/application has date and time entry fields. And, think about Time zone also.

- Make sure that Number/Currency/Name format is correctly displayed in all pages uniformly.

- When testing edit/modify/update feature, modify values of all fields and make sure that everything is getting updated correctly.

- Whenever testing Delete feature make sure that all the related data also getting deleted. For example, when deleting questions in a MCQ Quiz application, answers also will be deleted.

And, make sure that necessary constraints are enforced correctly. For example, deletion of questions should not be allowed if the questions are already used in some other modules.

Best practices in Software Testing

There are lots of materials available in internet to explain best practices in Software Testing.

Here I am writing only the very essential things for medium level projects based on my experience/view point.

- We should start our testing activities at beginning of Software development itself.
  Understanding **Scope/purpose** of the project will help to judge the degree/level of testing required.
- Testers should go thro' the requirements **in detail** without missing any points given by the client before writing test cases.
- The test cases should be **updated immediately** once the client gives new requirement or changes the requirements.
- The test case document should cover all the requirements even if some requirements are non-testable. These non-testable items should be marked as non-testable. Keeping **traceability matrix** document will helpful to achieve this.
- The Test case document should help to clearly **identify** hierarchy/arrangement of test cases. It should have clear approach to arrange test cases if many test cases exist with similar steps. It is not advisable to copy & paste the similar test cases many times, instead we can specify only the additional/different steps.
- **Description** of each test case should be written clearly after understanding the context/module of description. **Steps** should be written only after manually executing them. **Expected results** should not have any ambiguity. If required, Prerequisite/**preconditions** should be mentioned.
- Planning and creating **test plan** document is essential even for small short-term projects. The test plan document need not contain all the details, but it should contain at least very basic components such as scope, schedule, risks, environments, testers
- Planning of development/test/staging environments should be done clearly. And it is very important to move the code and maintain version of code in each environment without

any ambiguity/confusion. Testers should know which version of code/data is available in each environment

- Test execution should be done carefully based on the test cases. It is very important to use **appropriate test data**. It is better to create different set of test data during test case creation itself. The test data should cover valid format, invalid format and boundary values.

  Test result (pass/fail) should be clearly updated for each test case. It is good practice to mention **Actual behavior** if the test case fails.

  The test results should be communicated to the other parties (developers, business/client) daily even if all the test cases are not executed. In this case, we should add a note to indicate that the test execution is still in progress.

  The test execution summary document/mail should clearly mention date of execution, environment, test name and test result.

- In case, most of test cases are getting failed continuously, there is no meaning of continuing the execution. Execution should be resumed once after fixing the major issues.

- It will be nice if we highlight the testing status (**pass, fail, yetToStart**) in appropriate color.(i-e Pass in Green, Fail in Red and YetToStart in Blue) But anyway, just highlighting the test case with appropriate color without specifying status is not a good practice. Because while taking single color printout of the test report, it is difficult to see the status from the color.

- It is good practice to do some **adhoc** testing in addition to the test case execution.

- Clear/proper communication/co-ordination within the Testing team and also with other teams (developers, client/business) is very essential.

- The bug report should be prepared very **clearly** with all essential details, especially with the steps/testdata for reproducing the bug. The bug report should **help the developers** to reproduce the bug and to fix it.

- Doing **re-test** and small **regression test** is essential whenever a reported bug is fixed
- It is not good if we do all the testing manually, as manual testing will take more time/effort and it is difficult to manage, and also it not consistent or repeatable. So it is better to **automate** the test cases using test tools such as QTP (Quick Test professional). Even we can use simple shell scripts and vbscript to automate some part of the testing.

Importance of Software Test Automation using tools such as QTP

Software Testing plays an important role in Software Development lifecycle. Doing manual testing is not enough. We should go for Automation Testing also.

- *"To Error is Human"* is the fact which drives the need for automation testing. Because, manual testers may not execute the test cases correctly. There will be lot of possibilities for making mistakes. They may give **wrong input data** due to typo, or they may not notice the **actual behavior** of the system correctly, or they may not **report** the test result correctly, or they may miss to execute some test cases, or they may forget to run some preconditions, or they may change the sequence of test case execution in case sequence is important.
- Another important factor is, Automation test scripts will be used as a way of storing domain/project/task Knowledge gained by the Test Engineers. Say for example, if a Tester works in project for one year, he might have spent more time for learning the domain, purpose of the project, modules in the project, flow of all functionalities. He will be familiar with known issues and challenges.
  If this Tester leaves from the project, the knowledge gained

by him also will leave.

It is very difficult for the newly joining Tester to understand everything from the Test Case document.

If automation test scripts are already available then the new Tester can just start the testing by running the automation scripts, without gaining much knowledge about the project.

He can understand the flow/data by seeing the execution of the automation test scripts. But anyway, he should gain project/domain knowledge to enhance/update the automation scripts further.

So we can say that test automation is a way of **storing knowledge**.

- Automation tool such as QTP (Quick Test Professional) has feature for storing screenshot of each and every page navigated during the execution. So it can be used as a proof for completion of testing, and also we can refer the screenshots of previous executions if there is any need to refer them.
- Test report can be automatically written to a customized report page which will ensure accuracy of the report and also it can improve look & feel of the report.
- The very important advantage of automation testing over manual testing is **execution speed**. Test execution can be completed quickly and also we can execution the scripts in night time also without human involvement. So ultimately total time needed for testing can be reduced which will significantly help for timely project completion.
- There may be requirement of doing some testing at specific time. It can be easily achieved by putting execution of those automation test scripts in a task scheduler/crone job. The tool such as QTP supports automation object model to achieve this.
- The functional test automation scripts will be useful for doing performance testing also. Because many performance test tools will support reusing/calling of these test scripts.
- Some type of testing involves comparing large amount of data between previous version and current version as part of

regression testing. Practically it may not possible for doing it manually. This problem can be easily solved by simple shell script or any other scripts such as vbs, wsh.

- As the automation test tools support Data Driven Testing, Test execution can be done repeatedly with many different data sets.

There are lot of automation test tools are available for doing Functional, Regression and Performance Testing. Test complete, SilkTest, SilkPerformer, QARun, QALoad, TestPartner, WinRunner, LoadRunner, QTP, Rational Robot and openSTA are some of them. **QTP** is most widely used now as it supports vbscript and it can be used for testing many different applications just by adding required add-ins.

Need of Domain Knowledge for Software Testers

V-Model mandates the need for involvement of Software Testers from beginning of the Software Development life cycle. But in most of the cases, Software Testers are not having enough exposure to "business" background of the application. Just blindly writing (and executing)test cases by reading the business or functional requirements is not enough to test the application-under-test.

Software Testers should learn more about domain and background of the application. It will help them to understand the requirements in correct context, and will help to find any issue in the requirements itself.

Having enough business background knowledge will make the

Software Testers to act as effective bridge between the Business Analysts (BA) and the Developers.

Especially, Domain knowledge is very important for testing BFSI applications (Banking, Financial Services and Insurance).

Software Test Automation tool evaluation

In this chapter I will explain about **evaluating** Automation test tool and selecting appropriate tool suitable for our requirements. Before start evaluating tool we should analyze whether automating software testing will **really give any benefit** over manual testing for your needs.

Actually, **Software Test Automation** is a good way to cut down **time** and **cost**. But, it will reduce the **cost** and **time** only when it is really **necessary** or it is used **effectively**.

Test Automation is not required if you are going to use your application **one time only** or for **short period** only. For example, assume that you are having a website developed in ASP, and you are making some changes in this website. And, assume you are having solid plan for converting/migrating this ASP site into either ASP.NET or PHP in near future.

In this situation, it is not advisable to automate the testing of the new changes done in the ASP site. In this case, simply you can complete the testing **manually** and then you can start your automation testing preparation once after the migration is done.
So, basically we need to automate our testing procedure when we have lot of **regression** work.
Once after taking decision to do the test automation, the next step is selecting appropriate automation tool. There are hundreds of tools available for automating the software testing and some of them are

Free. Test complete, SilkTest, SilkPerformer, QARun, QALoad, TestPartner, WinRunner, LoadRunner, QTP, Rational Robot,Selenium,WATIR and openSTA are some of Test Automation Tools.

Some of these Tools (e.g *Selenium*) are open-sourced. We need to select appropriate tool based on below factors.

Budget allocated for the Testing process - Price for each automation tool will vary. Some of them are costly, and some of them are even free.
License pattern will be varying for each tool. License cost of some tools will vary according to geography location also. And, some tool vendors will fix different price for **seat license** and **floating license**.

So, first we need to decide about our licensing needs. i-e Ask below questions,
- In case the tool price changes according to geographic location, whether it will be cost effective for your location.
- How many Automation Test engineers will simultaneously work in your automation project?
- Whether you need separate set up for developing the scripts and for executing the scripts?
- Whether you are having plan to automate your any other testing activities? Whether the selected tool can be used for other projects also?

Support available for the Automation Tool. We need to evaluate whether the Tool provider will provide enough support and bug fix releases. And, we need to think about the support provided by the **Forum community** also.

Analyze whether the **execution speed** of the automation tool matches with your requirements.

Check the **installation requirements** (both Software and Hardware) for installing the automation tool in your test script development environment.

List down current **skill set of your testers** and check whether the tool can be effectively used by your testers. For example QTP will support vbscript, if your testers know vbscript they can easily learn using QTP.

Feasibility study is very important before finalizing the Tool. Most of Tools will provide evaluation or Trail offer. For example QTP can be downloaded from HP site and we can use it for 14 days. During this trial period try to automate different portions of your application to make sure that the Tool can be used for automating your Testing needs.

Analyze the Market Share and **financial Stability** of the vendor of the tool. It will get significance if you are going to use the Automation tool for long term regression testing purpose.

Check whether the Tool can be easily integrated with **bug tracking tools**. For example, QTP will be closely integrated with Quality Center (Test Director) which is a Test Management Tool.

The best approach is, we can **prepare a list** with all these factors and add remarks for each tool. And, we can select the tool by analyzing this list.

The need for having development/programming knowledge for Software Testers.

In this Chapter, I am going to write about the need for having basic **development** knowledge for **Software Testers**. I have worked as both Programmer and Software Tester. So, I think I will be the appropriate person for writing this Chapter.

When I worked as Programmer/developer, I used to see many **Software Testers** who used to create poor test strategy due to their poor programming knowledge. And, it may be difficult to set up proper **test environment** without having proper programming knowledge.

Assume that a Software Tester is going to test a Web application. If something goes wrong while doing his testing, he should be able to report the issue clearly by mentioning whether the error is happening from **client** (i-e browser) side, **network** connection or **server** side. It will help the developers to fix the issues quickly.

For doing this "narrow down", the Testers should know what is Client (webbrowser), how the server works and how internet is working. He should know how to see the client side error messages displayed by various browsers. Reproducing the issue also need some kind of development knowledge.

Being familiar with SQL and handling databases will help to test back end part of the web application. It will help to load some prerequisite data also to save testing time.

Test data collection task can be done easily if the Testers know little bit programming.

The recent **Agile development** model is trying to reduce the gap between Software Development and Software Testing.

So, I believe everyone will agree that it is very important to have programming knowledge if you are going to be a Software Tester.

Now, we can see how we can **give basic programming knowledge** to the Software Testers.

- Development Team can arrange session for giving overview about the development for the Software Testers.
- Software testers can start reading very basics of programming and web development from online tutorial sites such as w3schools.com
- Testers can participate in code review meetings.

Ok. This Chapter has explained the importance of having **programming knowledge** for the **Software Testers**. Similarly, it is important to have Software Testing knowledge for the programmers.

And, if your company is going to implement Test driven development, then it is important to have close interaction with the Development Team. This interaction will be effective only if the Software Testers are having some fundamental programming knowledge.

Software Testing Questions and Answers

Find the answers at the end of the questions.

1) The approach/document used to make sure all the requirements are covered when writing test cases
a) Test Matrix b) Checklist c) Test bed d) Traceability Matrix

2) Executing the same test case by giving the number of inputs on same build called as a) Regression Testing b) ReTesting c) Ad hoc Testing d) Sanity Testing

3) Control Charts is a statistical technique to assess, monitor, and maintain the stability of a process. a) True b) False

4) To check whether we are developing the right product according to the customer requirements are not. It is a static process a) Validation b) Verification c) Quality Assurance d) Quality Control

5) To check whether we have developed the product according to the customer requirements r not. It is a Dynamic process. a) Validation b) Verification c) Quality Assurance d) Quality Control

6) Staff development plan describes how the skills and experience of the project team members will be developed. a) True b) False

7) It is a set of levels that defines a testing maturity hierarchy a) TIM (Testing Improving Model) b) TMM (Testing Maturity Model) c) TQM(Total Quality Management)

8) A Non-Functional Software testing done to check if the user interface is easy to use and understand a) Usability Testing b) Security

Testing c) Unit testing d) Block Box Testing

---

9) The review and approved document (i.e. Test plan, System Requirement Specification's) is called as a) Delivery Document b) Baseline Document c) Checklist

---

10) What are the Testing Levels? a) Unit Testing b) Integration Testing c) System Testing and Acceptance Testing. d) All the above

---

11) Cost of quality = Prevention Cost + Appraisal cost + Failure cost a) True b) False

---

12) A useful tool to visualize, clarify, link, identify, and classify possible cause of a problem. This is also called as "fishbone diagram" what is this? a) Pareto Analysis b) Cause-and-Effect Diagram

---

13) It measures the quality of processes used to create a quality product.
It is a system of management activities,
It is a preventive process, It applies for entire life cycle & Deals with Process. a) Validation b) Verification c) Quality Assurance d) Quality Control

---

14) Variance from product specifications is called? a) Report b) Requirement c) Defect

---

15) Verification is
a) Process based b) Product based

---

16) White box testing is not called as_____
a) Glass box testing b) Closed box testing c) Open box testing d) Clear box testing

---

17) Name the events that will be analyzed, Count the named incidents, Rank the count by frequency using a bar chart & Validate reasonableness of the analysis is called as a) Pareto Analysis b) Cause and Effect Diagram c) SWOT Analysis d) Pie Charts

---

18) Retesting of a single program or component after a change has been made? a) Full Regression Testing b) Unit Regression c) Regional Regression d) Retesting

---

19) Requirement and Analysis, Design, Development or Coding, Testing and Maintenance is called as Software Development Life Cycle (SDLC) a) True b) False

---

20) The testing which is done by going thro' the code is known as, a) Unit Testing b) Blackbox testing c) White box Testing d) Regression testing

---

21) Configuration Management Plan describes the Configuration Management procedures and structures to be used. a) True b) False

---

22)This type of testing method attempts to find incorrect or missing functions, errors in data structures or external database access, interface errors, Performance errors and initialization and Termination errors. It is called as a) White Box Testing b) Grey Box Testing c) Black Box Testing d) Open Box Testing

23) Phase Definition. It will come under a) CMM Level 1 b) CMM Level 2 c) None

24) Software testing which is done without planning and Documentation is known as
a) adHoc Testing b) Unit Testing c) Regression testing d) Functional testing.

25) Acceptance testing is known as
a) Beta Testing b) Greybox testing c) Test Automation d) White box testing

26) Retesting the entire application after a change has been made called as? a) Full Regression Testing b) Unit Regression c) Regional Regression d) Retesting

27) Boundary value analysis belongs to which testing method?
a) Black Box testing b) White Box testing

28) It measures the quality of a product
It is a specific part of the QA procedure, It is a corrective process, It applies for particular product & Deals with the product. a) Validation b) Verification c) Quality Assurance d) Quality Control

29) What are the Types of Integration Testing? a) Big Bang Testing
b) Bottom Up Testing c) Top Down Testing d) All the above

30) Product Risk affects The quality or performance of the software.
a) True b) False

31) A metric used to measure the characteristic of documentation
and code called as a) Process metric b) Product Metric c) Test metrics

32) Which is non-functional software testing?
a) Unit Testing b) Block box testing c) Performance Testing d)
Regression

33) The process that deals with the technical and management issues
of software development called as? a) Delivery Process b) Testing
Process c) Software Process

34) Executing the same test case on a modified build called as a)
Regression Testing b) Retesting c) Ad hoc Testing d) Sanity Testing

35) Which is Black-Box Testing method?
a) equivalence partitioning b) code coverage c) fault injection

36) Business Risk affects The Organization developing or Procuring

the software. a) True b) False

---

37) Stratification is a Technique used to analyze/divide a universe of data into homogeneous groups (strata). a) True b) False

---

38) Automation Testing should be done before starting Manual testing.

Is the above statement correct?
a) Yes b) No

---

39) Earlier a defect is found the cheaper it is to fix it.

Is the above statement correct? a) Yes b) No

---

40) Informing to the developer which bug to be fix first is called as a) Severity b) Priority c) Fix ability d) Traceability

---

41) Software Testing is a process of evaluating a system by manual or automatic means and verify that it satisfies specified requirements or identity differences between expected and actual results. a) True b) False

---

42) Retesting modules connected to the program or component after a change has been made? a) Full Regression Testing b) Unit Regression c) Regional Regression d) Retesting.

---

43) An Important metric is the number of defects found in internal

testing compared to the defects found in customer tests, Status of test activities against the plan, Test coverage achieved so far, comes under a) Process Metric b) Product Metric c) Test Metric ⎯⎯⎯⎯⎯⎯⎯

44) Alpha testing will be done at,
a) User's site b) Developers' site

45) SPICE Means a) Software Process Improvement and Capability Determination b) Software Process Improvement and Compatibility Determination. c) Software Process Invention and Compatibility Determination. d) Software Process Improvement and Control Determination

46) Requirements Specification, Planning, Test case Design, Execution,
Bug Reporting & Maintenance This Life Cycle comes Under a) SDLC b) STLC c) SQLC d) BLC

47) It provides a set of levels and an assessment model, and presents a set of recommended practices that allow organizations to improve their testing processes. a) TIM (Testing Improving Model) b) TMM (Testing Maturity Model) c) TQM(Total Quality Management)

48) Standards and procedures for managing changes in an evolving software product is called? a) Confirmation Management b) Confederation Management c) Configuration Management d) Compatibility Management

49) Path Tested = Number of Path Tested / Total Number of Paths
a) True b) False

50) This Testing Technique examines the basic program structure
and it derives the test data from the program logic; Ensuring that all
statements and conditions executed at least once. It is called as a)
Block box Testing b) White box Testing c) Grey Box Testing d)
Closed Box Testing

51) This type of test include, how well the user will be able to
understand and interact with the system? a) Usability Testing b) User
Acceptance Testing c) Alpha Testing d) Beta Testing.

52) Defects generally fall into the following categories? a) WRONG
b) MISSING c) EXTRA d) All the above

53) What is correct Software Process Cycle? a) Plan(P)------
>Check(C)------>Act(A)----->Do(D) b) Plan(P)------>Do(D)------
>Check(C)----->Act(A) c) Plan(P)------>Do(D)------>Act(A)-----
>Check(C)

54) Conducted to validate that the application, database, and network
they may be running on can handle projected volumes of users and
data effectively. The test is conducted jointly by developers, testers,
DBA's and network associates after the system Testing called as a)
Functional Testing b) Stress/Load Testing c) Recovery Testing d)
Integration Testing

55) Maintenance Plan predicts the maintenance requirements of the system, maintenance costs and effort required a) True b) False

56) Beta testing will be done by
a) Developer b) User c) Tester

57) Validation plan describes the approach, resources and schedule used for system validation a) True b) False

58) Integration, It will come under a) CMM Level 1 b) CMM Level 3 c) CMM Level 2 d) None

59) Types of quality tools are Problem Identification Tools and Problem Analysis Tools. a) True b) False

60) Which Software Development Life cycle model will require to start Testing Activities when starting development activities itself a) Water falls model b) Spiral Model c) V-model d) Linear model

61) A metric used to measure the characteristic of the methods, Techniques and tools employed in developing, implementing and maintaining the software system called as a) Process metric b) Product Metric c) Test metrics

62) Check Sheet(Checklist) is considered a simple , but powerful statistical tool because it differentiates between two extremes. a) True b) False

---

63) Application should be stable. Clear Design and Flow of the application is needed for Automation testing. a) False b) True

---

64) Quality plan describes the quality procedures and standards that will be used in a project. a) False b) True

---

65) How severely the bug is effecting the application is called as a) Severity b) Priority c) Fix ability d) Traceability

---

66) Project Risk affects The Schedule or Resources. a) True b) False

---

67) The name of the testing which is done to make sure the existing features are not affected by new changes
a) Recursive testing b) Whitebox testing c) Unit testing d) Regression testing

---

68) Management and Measurement, It will come under a) CMM Level 1 b) CMM Level 3 c) CMM Level 4 d) CMM Level 2

---

69) AdHoc testing is a part of
a) Unit Testing b) Regression Testing c) Exploratory Testing d) Performance Testing

---

70) Cost of Production = Right The First time cost(RTF) + Cost of Quality. a) True b) False

---

71) ------------- means under what test environment(Hardware, software set up) the application will run smoothly a) Test Bed b) Checkpoint c) Code Walk through d) Checklist

---

72) TQM represents
a) Tool Quality Management b) Test Quality Manager c) Total Quality Management d) Total Quality Manager

---

73) Optimization, Defect Prevention, and Quality Control. Its come under the a) CMM Level 2 b) CMM Level 3 c) CMM Level 4 d) CMM Level5

---

74) Unit Testing will be done by
a) Testers b) End Users c) Customer d) Developers

---

75) Beta testing will be done at
a) User place b) Developers place

---

76) A Plan to overcome the risk called as a) Migration Plan b) Master plan c) Maintenance plan d) Mitigation Plan

---

77) Splitting project into tasks and estimate time and resources required to complete each task called as Project Scheduling a) True b) False

---

Answers

---

(1) d (2) b (3) a (4) b (5) a (6) a (7) b (8) a (9) b (10) d (11) a (12) b (13) c (14) c (15) a (16) b (17) a (18) b (19) a (20) c (21) a (22) c (23) b (24) a (25) a (26) a (27) a (28) d (29) d (30) a (31) b (32) c (33) c (34) a (35) a (36) a (37) a (38) b (39) a (40) b (41) a (42) c (43) c (44) b (45) a (46) b (47) a (48) c (49) a (50) b (51) a (52) d (53) b (54) b (55) a (56) b (57) a (58) b (59) a (60) c (61) a (62) a (63) b (64) b (65) a (66) a (67) d (68) c (69) c (70) a (71) a (72) c (73) d (74) d (75) a (76) d (77) a

QTP (i-e *Quick Test Professional*) is a **Test Automation Tool**. QTP is widely/most popularly used as Functional/Regression Test automation tool. It was initially developed by **Mercury Interactive** and then acquired by **HP (Hewlet-Packard)**.

Introduction to QTP

QTP supports external **add-ins**. So, it can be used for automating testing of many different software applications and websites. Some add-ins (e.g **ActiveX, VisualBasic, Web**) are built-in with QTP, and some other add-ins (e.g Java, .net, TE (terminal emulator))are external add-ins. **External add-in** means we need to install them separately once after installing QTP.

We have the option to load only the required add-ins when opening the QTP IDE. So, it will be helpful to improve the **execution speed**.

QTP supports **Keyword Driven testing** and **Data Driven testing**. We can create our own test automation framework (*Hybrid framework*) also based on our own requirements for test automation.

It is very important to understand **how QTP works**. Because it will help to learn any other features in QTP easily. And, it will help to design an effective **automation framework**. It will help to resolve any issue that may come across during automation script development and also during script execution.

It can be explained as below,
We know that every test case should have *Test Steps* and *Expected Results*. As QTP is used for executing these test cases, QTP also should have a way for handling both *Test Steps* and *Expected Results*.

Handling *Test Steps* means, QTP should be capable of navigating any path/page in any website or in any software application. For achieving this QTP should be able to **recognize** any **control/object** in any application/webpage which needs to be tested. For recognizing the object, it should know the **properties** of those objects beforehand. It is achieved by storing the properties of the objects in a centralized place known as **Object Repository.**

While running the test script, the objects in the application are identified/recognized by comparing the properties of the objects with the properties stored in the **Object Repository.** By doing this recognition, execution of Test Steps becomes possible.

QTP is having **Datatables** (similar to Excel sheet) for supporting execution for multiple iterations of same steps with different data. For example, assume that we need to execute two test cases, one for logging into a website using UPPER case username and another test case for logging into a website using lower case username.

For executing these two test cases, the steps will be same. The only difference is in the test data. It can be easily done in QTP by putting these input usernames in Datatable and make the Script to execute it two times.

Next, we need to think about handling *Expected Results*. The purpose of testing is comparing the Actual result with the predefined Expected Results. It is achieved by using **Checkpoints.**

There are many checkpoints available in QTP. They are **Standard Checkpoint, Text Checkpoint, Bitmap Checkpoint, Database Checkpoint, accessibility Checkpoint and XML Checkpoint.**

Actually QTP can be used simply as **Record and Play** type tool for automation of simple steps on simple applications. But it should be extensively used by writing user defined functions and many other features to get more benefit from it.

QTP is not using any Proprietary Script. It uses commonly available **VBscript**. So, writing script will be simple. And also, vbscript is commonly used in many places such as Web development (ASP), and in windows administration works. So we can easily find lot of already available user-defined functions and help articles in the Internet.

And, QTP supports **COM** model. i-e Any methods and properties of any COM based application can be easily accessed from QTP. For example IE(Internet Explorer) and Excel Objects can be created within QTP script. i-e IE can be opened from QTP itself using vbscript and the script can navigate to the desired URL and mostly it can do whatever we do manually in IE.
This COM support is applicable for QTP itself.
i-e Object of QTP itself can be created and handled. It is known as **Automation Object Model**. It will be useful for exporting the environment settings and also useful for scheduling the QTP scripts execution.

Basically, QTP is a functional/Regression testing tool. But it can be indirectly used for testing **performance** also. (*i-e QTP scripts can be called from performance testing tool "Load Runner"*). And, QTP is having limited performance testing options such as start and end transactions which will be helpful to find execution time for particular block of steps.

QTP can be closely integrated with the Test Management Tool **Quality Center (QC).** QC can be effectively used to run QTP scripts in multiple remote machines to complete execution of many test scripts in less time.

The user friendly IDE which has Keyword view, Expert view, Datatable, Active screen, object repository editor/manager, step generator, function generator, object highlight feature, intellisense, recovery scenario manager, update run feature and simple Test/Action handling features makes the Script developer/execution work easy. The IDE is integrated with useful tools such as ObjectSpy. The IDE has standard development features such as Debug

The below screenshot shows the appearance of QTP IDE.

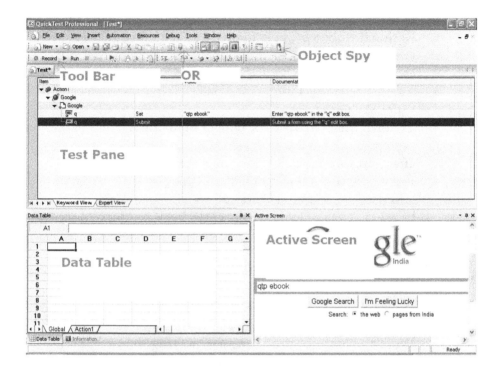

How to Learn QTP?

This chapter will give overview about learning QTP. You can read the details in coming chapters.

- Begin with understanding the importance of software testing. You should learn software testing Concepts and you have to get clear understanding of **functional and regression testing.** You need to be bit familiar with **Manual testing activities** such as **writing test cases, executing test cases** and **reporting the issues.**

- You have to understand the need and **importance of software test automation** before start learning QTP. Even having some basic knowledge about other Test automation tools such as **Test Complete, Test Partner, SilkTest** and **Rational Robot** will help to prepare Tool evaluation/selection document if you are going to use QTP as Test Automation Tool in your project.
- You can refer the **Tutorial** and other **Help files** installed with QTP installation.
- Try to understand basics of **Object repository**. You will become more familiar with using Object Repository once after start working on QTP automation.
- Familiarize yourself using **QTP add-ins** (i-e selecting/deselecting specific add-ins). Desired Add-ins can be selected while launching the QTP. Note that the add-ins enabled during recording should be enabled while running the script.
- Understand the basic units such as **Test, Actions** and **external vbscript** in QTP by going thro' the Help file and the Handbook document. Practice yourself by creating simple **Test** with one or two **Actions**.
- Practice yourself by **recording** and **playing** some steps using the sample application (*Flight booking Application*).
- Try to understand the need for having **multiple Actions** in a particular Test.
- Practice yourself **creating Actions** and **splitting** the Actions. And also, understand the need for having external reusable actions, and practice yourself using **"Call to Copy of Action"** and **"Call to Existing Action"**.
- Familiarize yourself with components such as **Expert view, keyword view, Active Screen** and **Datatable.**
- Learn basics of **vbscript** by going thro' the vbscript documentation available in QTP help file, and be familiar with syntax of frequently used vbscript functions such as **mid, instr** and **split.**
- Do some practice to have clear understanding of relation between **Test Objects** stored in object repository and the Vbscript statements showing in the **expert view**. You can do it by changing name of Test Object in OR and see the name

automatically got changed in the expert view statement. And also, you can try to add/remove/edit some properties of Test Object in the Object Repository.

- Understand the relationship between the **Keyword view** and the **expert view**. Both views are having their own advantages. So try to use both views. For example, Keyword view will be useful for doing parameterization easily and expert view can be useful or rearranging the steps.
- Learn different types of **Checkpoints** and use them in sample script developed using the sample application. Intentionally put wrong expected result in the checkpoints to see how the Test result will look when showing checkpoint failures.
- Learn to use multiple Object repositories (both Local and Shared), and also practice to get clear understanding of merging of Object Repositories.
- Learn **Recovery Scenario** to handle unexpected behavior of application. For learning Recovery Scenario you may need some application which shows a pop-up window rarely/randomly. Mostly you can use a website which is having both https and http links. Security alert will be shown while moving from https pages to http pages. You can use Recovery Scenario to handle this security alert window.
- Read the Help file to get clear understanding of Datatable and parameterization. And also learn about Action iteration and Test iteration without any ambiguity. Practice it by creating Data Driven testing for simple login screen.
- Start using Reporter.**ReportEvent** in the code to enhance the reporting of the results.
- Use **ObjectSpy** to get familiar with finding both TO properties and RO properties of the Object in the Application.
- Learn to change **Test Settings** and the **editor settings.** Here you should have clear understanding of which setting is applicable for the particular Test and which setting is applicable for particular instance of QTP installation.

- Understand the need for **Synchronization** and try to use different ways (*use of sync(), waitproperty, and exist*) to achieve it.
- Practice to use Step Generator, Function Generator and Active Screen to speed up the automation script creation process. Effective use of Active Screen will help you to continue your QTP script development even when your application is not available.
- Learn about different types of recording modes and understand the need for them. Low level recording may help you to handle some steps if the standard recording is not able to recognize the object using the currently available add-ins.
- Learn how to create/use COM objects such instance of Internet Explorer browser and an instance of excel object. It will be very useful.
- Learn to use Debug feature effectively. For example, use of "Run from step" will significantly reduce the Debug time.
- Understand the need for **Regular expression** and learn some frequently used regular expressions (e.g .*)
- Learn about **QTP automation framework** creation, and try to create a framework best suitable for your needs.
- Learn **Automation Object Model** and understand the need for them. For example Automation Object Model can be used for automatically start running QTP script at specified time.
- Learn about best practices (e.g always using **reference path**) and **coding standards**.
- Go thro' the QTP forums (e.g www.sqaforums.com) and read the discussions to get familiar with QTP issues and solutions/workarounds.
- Learn to connect with **database table** for checking the database content. For doing this either you can use **Database Checkpoints** or you can create script using **createobject.**
- Learn basics of **Descriptive programming (DP)** which is the alternative for Object Repository (OR). Personally I won't recommend to use DP because it will create maintenance problem. But anyway we need to learn Descriptive programming in case we need to update any existing DP code.

- Learn to integrate with **Quality Center (QC)** which is **Test Management Tool** provided by HP. It was formerly known as **"Test Director"**. We can execute the scripts from QC itself. And, it is used for maintaining Test cases and tracking Bug/Issues. Appropriate integration of QTP and QC will make Script maintenance, Execution and Reporting easy.

Understanding Object Repository

Object Repository is a centralized place for storing Properties of objects available in AUT (*Application Under Test*).

Why Centralized place? And, Why we should store the properties of objects available in AUT?
First, I will explain below things which will be helpful for understanding answers of above questions.

- All software applications and websites are getting developed using many different components or small units (*e.g textbox control in vb, input tag in HTML, webbrowser contorl in .net*) which can be called as Objects.
- Each object will be identified based on the object type. And also, each object will have its own properties (*e.g name, title, caption, color, size*) for helping to identify by each of them. And also, each object is having specified set of methods.
- Some of the properties can be changed during run-time. These are known as RO (Runtime object) properties. And some of them can not be changed. They are known as TO (Test Object) properties.
- You can use ObjectSpy available in QTP IDE to see the TO properties & methods and RO properties & methods of any object available in your application. (Make sure that required add-ins are available).

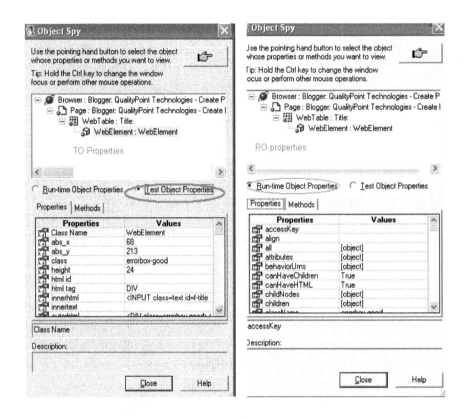

If you see TO and RO properties of many objects in different applications using ObjectSpy, you will be in a position to distinguish between TO and RO properties.

- Since TO properties are used for uniquely identifying any object, QTP will store only the TO properties of any object in the Object Repository.

- QTP will store TO properties of any object of AUT in Object repository as Name & Value pair. You can refer the below screenshot.

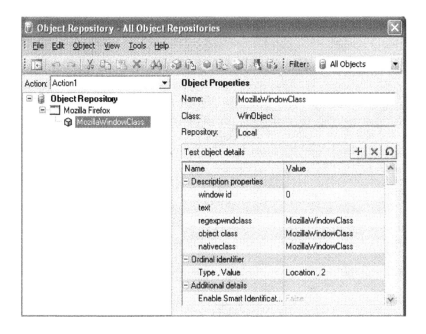

- The Objects stored in the Object repository(OR) are called as **Test Objects**. Actually it is just equivalent to the corresponding actual object in AUT.

- All the Test Objects that are stored in Object repository(OR) are arranged in a hierarchical structure. (e.g **Browser->Page->webelement**).

- QTP will store the TO properties of the Objects in many different ways.

- One simple way is, while doing Recording the TO properties will be stored to the OR.
- Second way is, TO properties can be stored by pointing the mouse cursor to required object in the AUT.
- Another way is manually adding the TO properties of the objects to the OR.

- Note that QTP won't store all the TO properties of the objects into the Object Repository. Only few properties will be stored to the OR, based on the setting done in **Object Identification window**. Refer the below screenshot. It can be opened from QTP IDE (Tools->Object Identification).

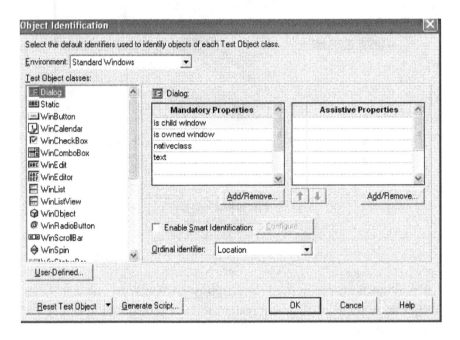

-Sometimes, QTP will store some additional properties such as index, location which are known as **ordinal identifiers**. Actually these properties **won't be available** in the object of AUT. It will be created by QTP automatically to distinguish two objects which are having exactly same TO properties. (e.g Some forms in the web pages will be have two submit buttons, one at top and another at bottom. QTP can identify them only based on location or index).

-Note that even QTP is storing TO properties based on properties of object of AUT (i-e real object), there is no need for all the TO properties to be available in RO properties collection also. (ie) QTP can derive (*i-e do some manipulation*) to get some new TO properties from one or many RO properties.

-Script can get TO properties of Test Objects using methods such as

getTOproperty and getTOproperties. Even, TO property of TestObject can be changed using **setTOproperty**. But anyway, it will be valid only till exiting the execution. After completing the execution it will resume the actual TO property stored in the OR.

During run-time we can get the property of the runtime object using **getROproperty.**

-Till this point we have seen about storing the Test Objects in Object Repository.

During Run mode, QTP will use these stored properties for comparing them with properties of actual objects of AUT to identify them.

- These Test objects can be represented in the script as ObjectType and Object name. (e.g *Window("Mozilla Firefox").Activate*).

- The object repository will support editing of properties of Test Object and new properties can also be added to them.

- The value for the properties of the Test Objects in OR need not be a constant. We can parameterize the values so that the TO property can be dynamically changed for each iteration of execution.

Now we can come to our Initial question. By storing properties in the centralized place, maintenance and updation of Test scripts can be easily done whenever there is a change in UI (User Interface) of the AUT.

Assume that Login screen is used in around 20 Test scripts. If the Page name of login screen in changed, we need not make any change in all these 20 Test scripts. Just changing the property of Test Object in OR is enough.

Clear understanding of Object Repository is essential if you are willing to use QTP extensively. Because we may face lot of difficulties/challenges while working with QTP. We should have clear knowledge in OR to face/solve them. Just Recording and Playback won't help much. And also, Test Automation framework can be done very effectively only when you are familiar with understanding/handling of Object Repository.

Different Types of Object Repositories

In this Chapter I will explain **various types** of Object repositories (OR).
You should be familiar with "What is **Test?**" and "What is **Action?**" in QTP for understanding the types of object repositories.

There are **two** types of Object Repositories available in QTP.

They are,

1. Local object Repository (Previously it was called as *per-action*)
2. Shared Object Repository.

Local Object Repository

Local Object Repository stores Test Objects in a file associated with each **Action**. i-e Each action will have its own local object repository.

These objects can be edited from the corresponding Action. This local object repository can NOT be used and/or edited by any other Actions within the same Test.

You can see separate **ObjectRepository.bdb** file inside each Action sub folder within the Test folder when you see them thro' windows explorer. The local object repository will be created automatically and the Test objects will be automatically stored in the Local repository while doing recording.

Shared Object Repository

A shared object repository stores test objects in a file(normally .tsr file) that can be accessed by **multiple Actions/Tests** in read-only mode.

We need to create this Shared Object Repository manually from **Object Repository Manager**.

We can export the local object repository objects into the Shared Repository file.

Associating Repositories

Each **Action** can use the objects from local object repository and from multiple shared object repositories.

Association of Object repositories can be done easily from the **"Associate Repositories"** Dialog window which will be opened from **Tools->Associate Repositories** menu in the Object Repository window.

By storing objects in shared object repositories and associating these repositories with Actions/Tests in your Test, you enable multiple Actions/Tests to use the objects.

It will improve maintenance of the script.

Since each Action is allowed to take objects from many places (*Local object repository and multiple Shared object repositories*), you should know how QTP will handle if object with same name is located in more than one repository.

QTP will give high priority to the local object repository. It will use the object from the Local object Repository if it finds object with same name in many repositories.

And, if more than one shared object repositories are having same object (i-e object with same name, properties may vary), QTP will use the object based on the order of association.

Since the shared object repository improves maintenance and enhances the re-usability, we should use them in our Automation project.

Local object repository can be used for learning purpose. Since they are getting created automatically, it will be easy to use for the beginners.

Understanding Action Iteration and Test Iteration

For beginners of QTP, it is very important to understand the difference between **Action** and the **Test**.

A QTP Test can have multiple Actions. The Actions can be arranged in **nested** manner (parent action-child action) also within the Test. Each Test will be stored as **QuickTest Test**. Actually it will be shown as Folder in windows explorer. Each Folder will have many files and many sub folders (one separate sub-folder for each Action).

Refer the below screenshot.

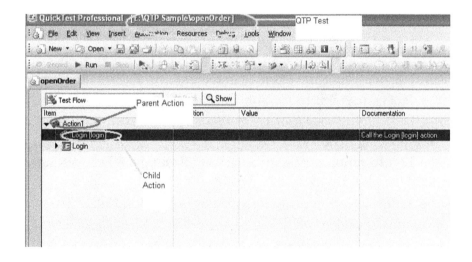

So it is clear that Actions are part of **Test**.

DataTables in QTP are used to enhance the script by doing Data-driven testing easily.

Refer the below screenshot.

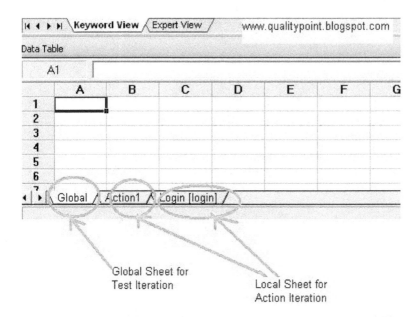

Global Sheet for
Test Iteration

Local Sheet for
Action Iteration

The Datatable is having One **Global Sheet** and several **local sheets** based on number of Actions used in the Test.

The Global sheet is used for storing the data used for Test Iteration, and the local sheets are used for storing the data related to corresponding Action iteration.

The **Test Iteration** can be specified from **Run tab of Test Settings** (File->Settings).

The **Action Iteration** can be specified from **"Action Call properties"** window which can be opened from Right click menu (context menu) of the particular Action.

Now the next step is when we should use both Test iteration and Action Iterations.

Assume that you are testing flight booking application which comes along with QTP installation.

You need to test different test cases of booking tickets 5 times.

So, we can easily do it by entering the ticket details in 5 rows of Action sheets and setting "Run on All Row" in "Action Call properties".

We know that we need to login into the application before booking Tickets.
So now the tickets will be booked 5 times with single user login.

Assume that we need to test this with 4 different users.
So, we need to book the tickets 20 (5x4) times.
It can be handled by using both Test Iterations and Action Iterations.
The user login details can be kept in the Global Sheet and the "Run on All Row" should be set in the Test settings.
So now script will execute 20 times to make 5 bookings with 4 user logins.

Recording Modes

Quick Test supports three different types of recording modes such as Normal mode, Analog mode and Low Level Recording mode.

Normal- QuickTest's normal recording mode records the objects in your application and the operations performed on them. This mode is the **default** and takes full advantage of QuickTest's test object model, recognizing the objects in your application regardless of their location on the screen.

In this normal mode the application/page will be recorded using relevant add-ins. For example, if you are recording a .net application, the objects will be recorded as Test objects specified in .net add-in. i-e the window will be recorded as **swfWindow.**

Analog – This mode records and tracks every **movement of the mouse**

This mode is useful for recording operations that cannot be recorded at the level of an object, for example, recording a **signature** produced by dragging the mouse.

We can record in Analog Recording mode **relative to the screen or relative to a specific window**.

The steps recorded using Analog Recording are saved in a separate data file.

Low level -records at the object level and records all run-time objects as Window or WinObject test objects.

Low Level Recording supports the following methods for each test object.

- o WinObject test object—Click, DblClick, Drag, Drop, Type
- o Window test object—Click, DblClick, Drag, Drop, Type, Activate, Minimize, Restore, Maximize

Run Modes

Normal -displays execution marker for showing the current execution step. It will be useful for debugging the script execution.

Fast- won't show the execution marker, so the execution will be faster than the normal run mode.

Update Run– QTP is having **Update Run** mode for updating test object descriptions, the expected checkpoint values, and/or the Active Screen images and values.

Choose **Automation >Update Run Mode** for running the scripts in update mode.

When QuickTest updates a test, it does not update parameterized values, such as Data Table data and environment variables.

CheckPoints

A *checkpoint* is a verification point that compares a current value for a specified property with the expected value for that property .

We can view the results of the checkpoint in the Test Results window.

Types of CheckPoints

We can add various types of checkpoints

- ➢ Standard check point
- ➢ Text check point
- ➢ Text area check point
- ➢ Bit map check point
- ➢ Data base check point
- ➢ Accessibility check point
- ➢ XML Check point (from Application)
- ➢ XML Check point (from Resource)
- ➢ Page check point
- ➢ Image checkpoint
- ➢ Table checkpoint

Standard Checkpoint checks the property value of an object in your application or Web page.

 The standard checkpoint checks a variety of objects such as buttons, radio buttons, combo boxes, lists, and so forth.

For example, you can check that a radio button is activated after it is selected or you can check the value of an edit box.

Image Checkpoint checks the value of an image in your application or Web page.

For example, you can check that a selected image's source file is correct.

Bitmap Checkpoint checks an area of your Web page or application as a bitmap

Useful for testing zoom of map and for testing logo.

Table Checkpoint checks information within a table.

Text Checkpoint checks that a text string is displayed in the appropriate place on a Web page or application

Accessibility Checkpoint identifies areas of your Web site that may not conform to the World Wide Web Consortium (W3C) Web Content Accessibility Guidelines (e.g Alt for Img tag)

Page Checkpoint checks the characteristics of a Web page. (e.g web page loading time, checking broken links)

Database Checkpoint checks the contents of a database accessed by your application.

XML Checkpoint checks the data content of XML documents in XML files or XML documents in Web pages and frames

Data Tables

QTP is having integrated Spread sheet (Excel). It is called as Data Tables. They are used for doing Data driven testing.

Data driven Testing is the process of Testing the same task with multiple sets of test data.

For example, we can test a login form by giving various usernames and passwords.

Two types of sheets in Data Tables.

There are two types of Data Sheets available within the QTP IDE.

1. Global Sheet - There will be one Global Sheet for the entire Test. i-e It will be used for all Actions in the test. Each row data will be taken based on the **Test** Iteration.

2. Action Sheets/Local Sheets- It will be applicable for the specific action only. Each row data will be taken based on the corresponding Action iteration.

Data can be imported to the Data Tables from external files (Flat files, excel sheets, etc) and Data bases (MS access, Sql Server, oracle, etc.)

QTP Result Window

Once after completing the script execution, QTP will generate the results in a hierarchy of tree structure. It will show the Checkpoint Results. And it will show the results from custom statements such as **Reporter.ReportEvent** also. Normally, it will be in **xml** format. We can save results as **HTML** file also. The result viewer is having option to filter the required results based on many criteria such as **pass, fail** and **warning**.

And, if we enable storing screenshots, the result window will show the difference between the Actual results and the Expected results in **visual** manner also. It will be easy to recognize any error in result screen.

Recovery Scenario

QTP is having a special feature called as **"Recovery Scenario"** for handling unexpected behaviors (e.g appearance of pop-up windows) of the application during the test execution.

We need to do **two steps** for using recovery Scenario. One is creating recovery Scenario file (.qrs file) and another step is associating the recovery scenario to the Tests.

We can use recovery scenario manager/wizard for creating recovery scenario file.

The **Recovery Scenario Wizard** allows you to create recovery scenario file by step-by-step process.

The Recovery Scenario Wizard contains five main steps

- ➢ Defining the **trigger event (Pop-up window, Object state, Test run error, Application crash)** that interrupts the run session
- ➢ Specifying the **recovery** operation(s) required to continue. We must define at least one recovery operation. And, we can add more than one recovery operations also.
- ➢ Choosing a **post-recovery** test run operation from the list of various options such as **Repeat current step and continue, Proceed to next step, Proceed to next action or component iteration, Proceed to next test iteration, Restart current test run, Stop the test run**
- ➢ Specifying a **name** and description for the recovery scenario.
- ➢ specifying whether **to associate** the recovery scenario to the current test and/or to all new tests

You open the Recovery Scenario Wizard by clicking the **New Scenario** button in the Recovery Scenario Manager Dialog box (**Resources > Recovery Scenario Manager**).

And, we can **associate** one or more scenarios with a test in order to instruct QTP to execute the recovery scenario(s) during the run session if a trigger event occurs.

We can add/Enable the required recovery scenario from the **Recovery Tab** of **"Test Settings"** window.

Any one of below options can be selected for activating the Recovery Scenario.

- **On every step**—The recovery mechanism is activated after every step.
- **On error**—The recovery mechanism is activated only after steps that return an error return value.
- **Never**

Synchronization

It is required to match execution speed of QTP with the loading/responding speed of application. Otherwise the test execution may fail at unexpected ways.

If you do not want QuickTest to execute a step or checkpoint until particular object in your application appears, you should insert a synchronization point to instruct QuickTest to pause the test until the object appears (or until a specified timeout is exceeded).

You can add synchronization point from menu (**Insert > Synchronization Point**) after start recording the test.

And, we can use **Exist** or **Waitproperty** statement for providing synchronization.

Automation Object Model

Just as we use QTP to automate testing of our application, we can use Automation Object Model (AOM) of QTP to automate QTP operations.

Using the objects, methods, and properties exposed by the QuickTest automation object model, we can write programs that configure QuickTest options and run tests or components instead of performing these operations manually using the QuickTest interface.

We can see **Generate Script** button in the Properties tab of the Test Settings dialog box, the General tab of the Options dialog box, and the Object Identification dialog box. Clicking this button generates an automation script file (**.vbs**) containing the current settings from the corresponding dialog box.

The generated script will follow the Automation Object Model and it will be useful for transferring setting in one instance of QTP into other instances.

For example, assume that you are working in your local computer , and you made some changes in the QTP interface. Once you complete your development in your local machine I will move the scripts to your customer machine. The script may NOT work in your customer machine. In this case we need to use this generated script to keep same settings in your customer machine also.

AOM scripts are useful for scheduling QTP script executions. We will see about this in another chapter.

Handling Passwords in QTP Scripts

Most of the applications/websites will require a password for getting into them. So, automation tools such QTP should be able to handle the passwords. But anyway, it is not a good practice to keep the password as it is in the scripts.

By default QTP will **encrypt** the password while recording. The recorded step will look like the below statement.

*Dialog("Login").WinEdit("Password:").**SetSecure** "49ff257067d53a774881c348da151ccf9282c2109b60"*

SetSecure method will be specifically used for handling passwords.

This recording approach will be useful only when you are going to use one or few passwords in your script.

If you want to use many number of different passwords for executing many iterations, this recording approach won't be much useful.

In this case we can use **password encoder** utility provided by QTP.

It can be accessed from start menu (*e.g Programs->Quick Test Professional->Tools->Password Encoder*)

It will look like below screenshot.

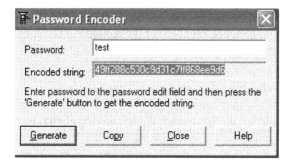

We need to enter the password text, and clicking "Generate" button will provide the encoded password string. We can put this string in the Datatable for executing multiple iterations with different passwords.

It will be useful not only for automating the testing, but also in below scenario.
- you want to allow a person available in a remote place to get into your application/site for doing some testing or for some other purpose, and you don't want to share the password with him. In this case you can just create a QTP script to log into the application.

Some people may not be willing to store the password in the QTP script even in the encrypted form also.

In this case, we can create a simple HTML form and call it from QTP script to show as a pop-up window for getting password from user while executing the Script.

It is possible to see the encrypted password in plain text format. So, don't store your important passwords in encrypted format also. Instead of storing the password, you can create a simple HTML form and call it from QTP script to show as a pop-up window for getting password from user while executing the Script.

Below lines of code were created while recording the login window of the sample flight application using QTP.

Dialog("Login").WinEdit("Agent Name:").Set "quality"

Dialog("Login").WinEdit("Password:").SetSecure "4ce5631fdebb5762c2878e 6f8f735a9d0511b0b7"

Here we can see the encrypted value
"4ce5631fdebb5762c2878e6f8f735a9d0511b0b7" for the password
"mercury"

But, when I run the QTP script after just changing the code like
below, I was able to see the plain text password "mercury" in the
Agent Name field.

Dialog("Login").WinEdit("Agent Name:").SetSecure "4ce5631fdebb5762c28
78e6f8f735a9d0511b0b7"

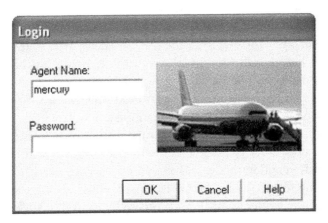

Required Steps/Processes in QTP Automation

- Before starting actual automation task, we should do **tool
  evaluation** and **feasibility study** to make sure QTP is the
  appropriate tool for automating test cases of our application.
  It can be done by selecting few sample
  modules/screens/flow from the application/test cases and
  create simple QTP scripts to make sure QTP will recognize
  the objects in our application

- As part of **Test driven development**, we can ask the application development team to give proper name or any other identification properties for the objects, if our feasibility study reveals some difficulty for QTP to recognize the objects.
- As I mentioned earlier, we should start our actual automation work only after completing some basic manual testing to make sure the application is **stable** and in working condition.
- QTP developers should review the Test cases and update it to specify which test cases can be automated and which can not be automated. Because ideally it is not possible to automate all the test cases. Difficulty in navigation or object identification issue or difficulty in verifying the result will prevent automation. If possible, the manual test cases can be rearranged to have separate **automation test cases**.
- Once after reviewing all the test cases and after getting familiar with the application we can design the **automation frame work** for our need
- Keep **separate instance** of application specifically for the purpose of developing automation scripts. It will avoid any unnecessary mess up with manual testing processes.
- Set up proper QTP development environment with **required Add-in** and with any add-in extensibility. If many people are going to involve in the development activities then we need to clearly document the responsibility of each person and the approach for sharing the scripts. If application is installed in remote machine then QTP also should be installed in remote machine. Because QTP will not recognize the objects of application in remote session.
- Set up proper object identification properties in QTP IDE.
- Once after completing all the above basic steps, the first development task should be adding all the required Test Objects/properties to the **Object repository.** It can be done by recording or by manually adding the objects to Object repository. If you specify any object using DP (Descriptive Programming) remember to document it.
- Once after adding all the objects, **rename** them to have unambiguous/meaningful name. Doing renaming from object repository will automatically change the name of the

object in the script also. But reverse is not true. I-e Renaming a object from script won't automatically change it in Object repository.

- Based on your design of automation framework, create **reusable actions** and vbscript functions using step generator or keyword view or expert view or using Active screen.
- Using these reusable actions prepare a **sample/base script** for executing few test cases. And then test it to make it error free.
- Once after completing the above mentioned sample script, do **parameterization** (data driven testing) for executing multiple iterations. Parameterization can be easily done from both keyword view and expert view.
- Add **checkpoints** to verify the expected results. Make sure that your checkpoints will work with different data. i-e use **regular expressions** if some part of expected value will change based on the input data during each iteration of test execution. And, editing checkpoint in QTP is having some issues. So, take care when editing the checkpoint. Mostly changing checkpoint in one place will affect the other checkpoints also. Or, you can create your own functions for creating checkpoints.
- Use appropriate **Regular expression** to make sure the script runs in all scenarios even when some properties are getting changed dynamically in particular pattern. For example if your screen page title changes based on the username of the logged in user, the script will not work correctly for all users. (By assuming that the script uses the page title for identifying the screen). You can refer the QTP help files if you don't know how to add Regular expression.
- Add the **Recovery scenarios** to handle any unexpected behavior of the application. Recovery scenario manager and wizards
- Use **Environment variables** to avoid any hard coded values in the script.
- Do dry run for this sample script and **debug** the issues in the automation script and fix them

- Do the above steps for **all the test cases**
- Create a **Driver script** which will call all the test scripts. Need to take additional care about deciding whether driver script should take data from its own datasheet or whether it should read data from Datatable of the called action.
- Complete **dry run** for the Driver script. It is really a challenging task. Because most of the Actions within the Driver script will depend each other and it will take very long time to complete the dry run if we start the dry run from starting point every time whenever the script fails in between the execution. I will explain with one example. Assume that your driver script calls three Tests. First Test will create a user account, second will test the Profile update feature, and third one will test the user deletion feature. And, assume that the second Test will use the user name created by First test, and the third test deletes the account created by first Test. In this scenario, if you face any difficulty while calling second test we need not always start the dry run from beginning. Since one user account was already created by first Test successfully, we can just comment out the calling of first Test and then continue the debugging of second Test using the already created account.
- Prepare .vbs script using **Automation Object Model** to run the QTP scripts in other environments also with same settings. It can be easily done by using "Generate script" option in QTP IDE.
- **Run** the scripts in desired environment.
- **Analyze** the test results.
- **Report** the bugs/defects in the application once after completing the analysis.
- Once after completing functional testing, select few essential scripts and store them separately for the future Regression Testing.

Best Practices in QTP Automation

- Start your automation work only when AUT (Application Under Test) is **stable**. i-e You should have completed initial round of manual testing before starting QTP automation task.
- Use reusable actions wherever possible. And, Functional libraries should be used to include the vbscript functions so that maintenance of vbscript functions is easy.
- Don't copy and paste checkpoints when you wish to check same thing in more than one places. Instead, create separate checkpoints. Because manipulating checkpoints in QTP is not feasible or it will be difficult.
- Open browser/application after opening QTP.
- Your vbscript functions should not have any hard coded object names, the name of the objects should be passed as function argument.
- Use **Shared** Object Repository. My suggestion is, don't use DP (Descriptive Programming) which will increase your maintenance work.
- Before adding any object to Object Repository, set up appropriate object identification properties (in Tools->ObjectIdentification) if you feel that default identification properties are not suitable for you application. If you do it after adding some objects to the Object Repository then you may face issues related to having multiple Test objects in Object Repository for a single actual Object.
- Open QTP using **Automation object model**. You can do it just by writing (*even you are having 'generate script' option in the QTP IDE itself*) simple .vbs file, and then open QTP just by double clicking this .vbs file. It is very essential if you are developing your scripts in one machine/environment and planning to run/execute it in another environment. By using Automation Object model we are making sure that all the IDE settings (e.g Object identification properties) that are

changed in development environment are propagated to the execution environment also

- Always use **Reference/Relative path** when calling any external reusable action instead of using absolute/full path, Otherwise the script will fail when placing it in different path.
- Remember to take **backup** of Object Repositories before merging object repositories.
- Put proper inline **comments** and also put summary comments (*description, input & output parameters, dependency, and author*) at beginning of the Test. In the comments remember to mention about execution/data flow.
- **Rename the Objects** in Object Repository to have proper meaning for them. Because the default name given by adding the objects by recording or manually may not be good/meaningful.
- Give attention to **synchronization** (i-e use of sync, waitproperty, exist). And also use regular expression wherever required. Otherwise consistency of script execution will be affected.
- Use **recovery scenario** to handle any unexpected behaviour (*e.g showing pop-up windows sometimes*) of the application.

Scheduling QTP Script Execution .

Once after successfully completing **dry run** of QTP scripts there is no need to monitor the script execution. We can schedule the script execution during night time also.

Scheduling can be done easily using **window task scheduler** for starting the execution of QTP script **automatically** at a predefined time.

For doing scheduling, we need to create **.vbs file.**
The Important steps required for scheduling are,

- Create a **Driver script** which calls all the scripts one by one.
- Complete **Dry run** to make sure script will continue execution without any interruption. Add Recovery scenario for handling any

unexpected pop-up window or any other inconsistent behavior of the application under test.

- Create a .vbs file which will be used for starting the QTP using Automation Object Model. Remember to add the code for keeping settings/options of the QTP so that the scheduler will open QTP with same settings.

you can refer the below sample vbscript code for creating the .vbs file to be called from the scheduler.

```
'Declare the Application object variable
Dim qtApp As QuickTest.Application
'Declare a Test object variable
Dim qtTest As QuickTest.Test
' Declare a Run Results Options object variable
Dim qtResultsOpt As QuickTest.RunResultsOptions
' Create the Application object
Set qtApp = CreateObject("QuickTest.Application")
' Start QuickTest
qtApp.Launch
qtApp.Visible = True
'Open the test in read-only mode. Include your driver script here.
qtApp.Open "C:\Tests\Test1", True
' Create the Run Results Options object
Set qtResultsOpt = CreateObject("QuickTest.RunResultsOptions")
' Set the results location qtResultsOpt.ResultsLocation =
"C:\Tests\Test1\Res1"
' Run the test
qtTest.Run qtResultsOpt
```

The complete code and details can be found in the QTP help file for Automation Object Model.

The next step is, we should merge the code for QTP options/settings within this code.

The options/settings code can be easily generated automatically.

Click **Tools->Options** from QTP IDE to open the below screen.

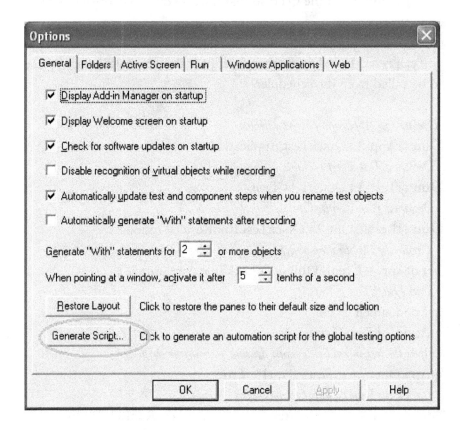

Click "generate" in the above screen to automatically generate the code.

- Then add a task in windows scheduler for calling the .vbs file.

You can do it by using Schedule Task wizard from **settings-**

>control panel->Scheduled Tasks->Add Scheduled Task

Click "Browse" in the below screen of the wizard to set specify your .vbs file.

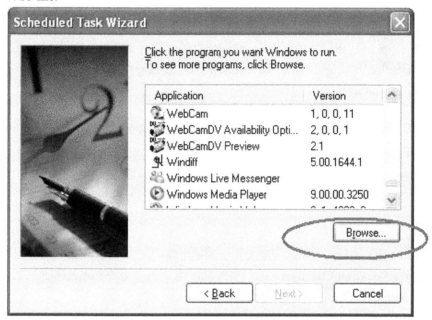

- Locking the system while running the script will affect the script running. So don't lock your machine while running the script. Anyway, you can add the below code at end of your .vbs file to lock the system automatically once after completing execution of the script.

Set obj = **CreateObject**("WScript.Shell")
sCmnd = "%windir%\SYSTEM32\rundll32.exe
user32.dll,LockWorkStation"
obj.**Run** sCmnd, 0, **False**

Basics of vbscript

VBscript is the scripting language used in QTP. It is developed by Microsoft. **VBscript** is subset of VB (Visual Basic) and VBA(Visual Basic of Applications). VBscript is used by other technologies also. For example, it is used in **ASP** (Active Server Page) for web site development. So we will be getting more ready-made functions/code written in vbscript from the Internet. It will save QTP script development time.

VBscript will access the host/system thro' Microsoft's **Windows Script Host (WSH)**. We can use WSH scripts also in QTP. It can be effectively used to automate the Test scenarios such as rebooting the system automatically after doing some steps and locking the system automatically.

QTP recording feature will automatically generate VBscript code while recording the steps. And, QTP IDE is having **"Function Generator"** for creating the vbscript functions.

VBScript Variables
In VBScript, all variables are of type *variant*, that can store different types of data.
Rules for VBScript variable names:

- Must begin with a letter
- Cannot contain a period (.)
- Cannot exceed 255 characters

dim will be used for declaring the variable as below.
Dim TestCaseID

The value for this variable can be assigned as below
TestCaseID="TC1"

84

Remember to use **option explicit** at top of your script. Otherwise a new variable will be created automatically if you misspell the variable name when assigning value for it.

We need to understand **scope/lifetime** of variable clearly. A variable declared within a function will exist only within that function. That means the variable will be destroyed when exiting the function, and more than one function can have variable with same name. So it is called as **Local variable**.

So, it is very important to have clear understanding about the **scope/lifetime** of variable declared/used in **Test/Action/function library/datatable/environment.**

Array variable can be declared as below.
Dim ArrIDs(10)
The above declaration will create single-dimension array containing 11 elements. i-e the array in vbscript is 0 based.

Operators

Arithmetic

Description	Symbol
Exponentiation	^
Unary negation	-
Multiplication	*
Division	/
Integer division	\
Modulus arithmetic	Mod
Addition	+
Subtraction	-
String concatenation	&

Comparison

Description	Symbol
Equality	=
Inequality	<>
Less than	<
Greater than	>
Less than or equal to	<=

Greater than or equal to	>=
Object equivalence	Is

Logical

Description	Symbol
Logical negation	Not
Logical conjunction	And
Logical disjunction	Or
Logical exclusion	Xor
Logical equivalence	Eqv
Logical implication	Imp

VBScript Procedures

In VBScript, there are two types of procedures:

- Sub procedure
- Function procedure

A Sub procedure:

- is a series of statements, enclosed by the **Sub** and **End Sub** statements
- **does not return** a value
- can take arguments

- without arguments, it must include an empty set of parentheses ()

eg.

```
Sub displayName()
  msgbox("QualityPoint Technologies")
End Sub
```

or

```
Sub addvalues(value1,value2)
  msgbox(value1+value2)
End Sub
```

When calling a Sub procedure you can use the Call statement, like this:

Call MyProc(argument)

Or, you can omit the Call statement, like this:

MyProc argument

A Function procedure:

- is a series of statements, enclosed by the **Function** and **End Function** statements
- **can return** a value
- can take arguments
- without arguments, must include an empty set of parentheses ()
- returns a value by assigning a value to its name

Find below a Sample function.

```
Function addvalues(value1,value2)
    addvalues=value1+value2
End Function
```

The above function will take two arguments and will add those two values and then it will return the sum value. Note here the sum value is returned by assigning it to the function name.

The above function can be called as below.

```
msgbox "Sum value is " & addvalues(1,2)
```

Conditional Statements

In VBScript we have four conditional statements:

if statement - executes a set of code when a condition is true

```
(e.g) if i=10 then
        msgbox "I am 10"
      End if
```
if...then...else statement - select one of two sets of lines to execute
```
(e.g) if i=10 then  msgbox "I am 10"
      else msgbox "other than 10"
      end if
```

if...then...elseif statement - select one of many sets of lines to execute

```
(e.g) if i=10 then  msgbox "I am 10"
      elseif i=11 then msgbox "I am 11"
      else msgbox "unknown"
      end if
```

select case statement - select one of many sets of lines to execute

```
select case value
case 1
  msgbox "1"
case 2
  msgbox "2"
case 3
  msgbox "3"
case else
  msgbox "other than 1,2 and 3"
end select
```

Looping Statements

Use the **For...Next** statement to run a block of code a specified number of times.

```
e.g
for i = 0 to 5
  msgbox("The number is " & i )
next
```

If you don't know how many repetitions you want, use a **Do...Loop** statement.

The Do...Loop statement repeats a block of code while a condition is true, or until a condition becomes true.

Built-in Functions

VBscript is having many useful built-in functions.

inStr, isNull, LCase, Left, Len, Mid, Now, Replace, Split, UBound, CStr, CreateObject, Date and DatePart are functions that are most frequently used in QTP script development.

KeyWord Driven Testing and Framework in QTP

Keyword-driven testing is a Software testing technique that separates much of the programming work from the actual test steps so that the test steps can be developed earlier and can often be maintained with only minor updates, even when the application or testing needs change significantly. In case of keyword driven testing, we need to do proper planning and initial huge effort. Anyway it will give benefit of easy maintenance and easily adding more test cases/scenarios.

As we see the keyword view in QTP IDE, the keyword driven testing involves specifying the test steps in below format

Object Action *parameter*

e.g
Browser("FireFox").Page("QualityPointHome").webEdit("us ername").Set "QualityPoint"

Here,

->Browser("FireFox").Page("QualityPointHome").webEdit("username") is the Object.
->"Set" is the Action.
->"QualityPoint" is the parameter.

Here we can change any of the three things to create test steps.

The **Keyword Driven framework** consists of the basic components given below

1. Control File
2. Test Case File
3. Startup Script
4. Driver Script
5. Utility Script

1. Control File

a) Consists details of all the Test scenarios to be automated.

b) User will be able to select a specific scenario to execute based on turning **on** or **off** a flag in the Control File.

c) Control File is in the form of an excel worksheet and contains columns for Scenario ID, Execute (Y/N), Object Repository Path, Test Case File Path.

2. Test Case File

a) Contains the detailed steps to be carried out for the execution of a test case

b) It is also in the form of an excel sheet and contains columns for Keyword, Object Name, Parameter

3. Startup Script

a) The Startup script is utilised for the initialization and reads the control files.

b) It then calls the driver script to execute all the scenarios marked for execution in the control file.

4. Driver Script

a) It Reads the Test Case files. Checks the keywords and calls the appropriate utility script functions based on specific keyword

b) Error Handling is taken care of in the driver script.

5. Utility Scripts

a) Perform generic tasks that can be used across applications.

Advantage of keyword Driven Framework.

• The main advantage of this framework is the low cost for maintenance. If there is change to any test case then only the Test Case File needs to be updated and the Driver Script and Startup script will remain the same.
• No need to update the scripts in case of changes to the application.

The framework design will be purely based on your requirements and your way of thinking. There is no Solid rule to follow.

Personally, I would like to have my own framework (hybrid framework) designed according to my own requirements.

Anyway, the best practice is, we should create below sub folders in your root folder.

ObjectRepository-> To keep your shared object repositories.
Datatables->To keep QTP data tables and external Excel sheets.
Config-> To keep environment variable xml file
RecoveryScenario ->To keep your recovery scenario files.
Tests-> You can keep your QTP Tests here. You may include Test containing Reusable Actions here. And a Test which is getting used as driver script can also be stored here.
library->you can keep your vbs file which contains vbscript functions.
Results-> You can store Result files (Either QTP result file or customized result file) here.
Actually there won't be any solid rules/approach for creating QTP framework.

Descriptive Programming in QTP

Instead of using Object Repository for storing properties of Test objects, we can straight-away define the properties while writing the script itself. It can be done in two ways.

One is, by giving the description in form of the string arguments.

For example a text box having html code as <input type="text" name="txtUser"> can be accessed as below.

Browser("Browser").Page("Page").WebEdit("Name:=txtUser","html tag:=INPUT").set "QualityPoint".

The other way is using Decription.create as below.

Set objDesc = Description.Create

objDesc("html tag").value= "INPUT"

objDesc("name").value= "txtUser"

Browser("Browser").Page("Page").WebEdit(objDesc).set "QualityPoint".

This Descriptive approach is having some short-comings.

The main **disadvantage** of Descriptive programming is **Maintenance** issue.
Since Object repository will be stored in centralized place, property definition for any Object can be easily changed at any time if the application developer changes the property of the actual object/control.

But, in descriptive programming (DP) it is difficult to change the object property as each QTP developer will be defining object property in many places using DP.

For example, assume that you and team member are developing

automation test scripts for testing gmail application.

Gmail login script will be used in many test scenarios.

Assume that you are automating some scenarios and your team member is automating some other scenarios.
In case of Object Repository, you and your team member will be forced to use same object description for login page controls/Objects (e.g username, password, login button).

So in future if Google changes any property (e.g change the button name from "login" to "get into gmail"), all the scenarios can be easily updated just by updating this change in Object repository.

But in case of DP, there is a possibility of defining the login button in multiple places. One definition by you and another by your team. (Anyway proper Team Coordination will avoid this issue, but practically it is very difficult to achieve this coordination.).

So, comparatively updating DP style coding is bit difficult if the application properties got changed.

Anyway, Descriptive programming is having its own **advantages** as mentioned below.

1. We can start work on writing QTP scripts even before the application under Test is NOT available. It will help to increase the utilization of the Automation scripts as it will be immediately available once the application gets released.

2. We can define the properties of an object without considering the

parent objects in the hierarchy. i-e Object identification will not depend on its parent object.

Managing Object Repositories in QTP

QTP is having separate window named as **"Object Repository Manager"** for managing various object repositories.

You can open this window from the Menu **"Resources->Object Repository Manager..."**

The **Object Repository Manager** enables you to manage all of the shared object repositories used in your organization from a single, central location.
It will be used for adding and defining objects, modifying objects and their descriptions, parameterizing repositories to make them more generic, maintaining and organizing repositories, **merging** repositories, and importing and exporting repositories in **XML format**.

The **Object Repository Manager** window will look like below one.

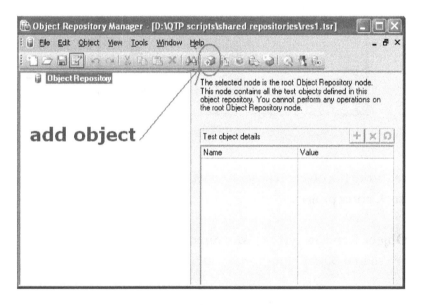

You can create new shared repository from this window and can store it as **.tsr** file.

While adding objects, you will be provided with two options. Either you can choose to add **only** the selected Object or you can choose to add the selected object and its **descendants**.

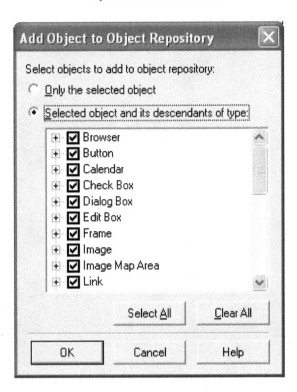

You can store the object repositories either in **file system** or in **Quality Center** project.

The **Object Repository(OR) Manager** enables you to open multiple shared object repositories and modify them as needed.

This Object Repository Manager provides the options such as **"Add objects"**, **"Highlight in Application"**, and **"Locate in Repository"** for the Shared object repository. It is similar to the local object repository. I will be explaining them in separate post.

By default this **OR Manager** will be in readonly mode. i-e you can not edit anything in this mode.

We need to choose **File>Enable Editing** for making it editable.

Update from Local Repository option in the OR Manager (**Tools > Update from Local Repository**) can be used for merging objects from the local object repository of one or more actions to a shared object repository.

And, it provides **Object Repository Merge Tool** for merging two shared object repositories.

At the end of the merge process, the **Object Repository Merge Tool** provides a graphic presentation of the original objects in both repositories, which remain unchanged, as well as the objects in the merged target object repository.

Objects that had conflicts are highlighted. The conflict of each object that you select in the target object repository is described in detail. **The Object Repository Merge Tool** provides specific options that enable you to keep the suggested resolution for each conflict, or modify each conflict resolution individually, according to your requirements.

And note that while the Object Repository Merge Tool is open, you cannot work with the Object Repository Manager.

Apart from this OR Manager, QTP is having **"Associate Repositories"** option for enabling you to associate one or more shared object repositories with one or more actions in a test.

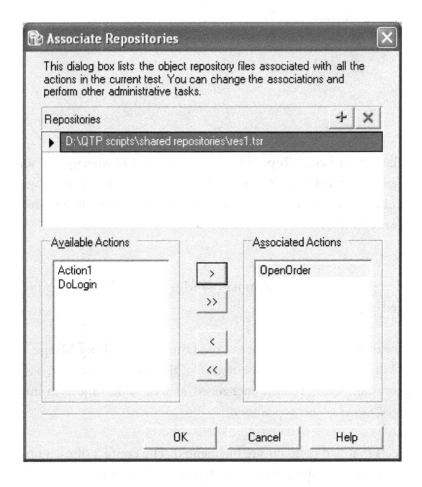

Object Spy in QTP

QTP is having a Tool called as **"Object Spy"** for viewing the **properties** and **methods** of any object in an open application.

We can use the Object Spy pointer (a button with hand symbol) to point to an object in the application.

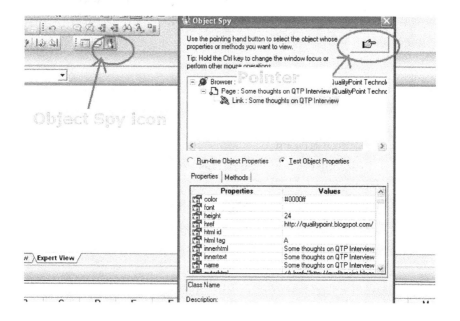

Object Spy Dialog window is having Two Tabs. One is "**Properties Tab**" and another is "**Methods Tab**".

Each tab is having **radio button** to choose one of two options "Run-Time Object" and "Test Object".

The **Object Spy** displays the selected object's **hierarchy tree** and its properties and values in the **Properties tab** of the Object Spy Dialog box.

The Object Spy enables you to view both the run-time object methods and the test object methods associated with an object in the **Methods tab** of the Object Spy dialog box.

And, we can to view the syntax for a selected method.

We can bring the **"Object Spy"** by clicking the **Tools->Object Spy...** menu or by clicking a toolbar button (an icon showing a person with hat). This icon can be accessed from **Object Repository** window also.

To see the properties of an object, first click on the button showing hand symbol in the Object spy Dialog.

The mouse pointer now changes in to a **hand symbol** and we have to point out the object to spy the details about the object.

If the required object is not visible, or window is minimized then hold the **Ctrl Key** and activate the required window to bring the required window to the front.

Then release the **Ctrl button** to make the cursor again **hands symbol** so that you can point the required object.

QTP methods and script for reading object properties

In the previous Chapter, I had written about Object Spy. For using **Object Spy**, we need to point the Object Spy pointer on the Object.

i-e We can read the properties **manually** only. And it can be done in the design time only.

In this post, I am going to write about reading the properties of any Object in the application using **scripting** (i-e programmatically in run-time)

QTP is supporting below methods.

GetTOProperty- This method returns the value of the property from the test object's description, i.e., the value used by QTP to identify the object. In other words the list of properties stored the Object Repository. If the property is not part of the test object's description, a warning will be issued by QTP.

GetTOProperties - This method is similar to GetTOProperty, but it will list all/collection of properties and their values.

It can be used as below to get all the Test Object properties and their values in "Submit" button of "Login" window in a vb application.

Set theTestObject = VbWindow("Login").VbButton("Submit")

Set Props = theTestObject.GetTOProperties

PropsCount = Props.Count

For i = 0 To PropsCount - 1

   PropName = Props(i).Name

   PropValue = Props(i).Value

   MsgBox PropName & " = " & PropValue

Next

GetROProperty - It will be used to get the value of an object property during **runtime**, such as the current list/combo item selection, page title, or the text in a WebEdit, or the size (width & height) of an object.

SetTOProperty changes the value of a test object property.

Changing the property won't make any change in the Object Repository, but it will just affect the way QTP identifies the object during runtime. Actually, this changes the properties of the temporary copy of the object stored in RAM by QTP.

i-e QTP is having the methods **GetTOProperty**, **GetTOProperties** and **SetTOProperty** for handing Test Objects.

And, it is having **SetTOProperty** method for handing Run-time object.
Obviously it can not have method SetROproperty, because QTP script should not change the actual objects (*But still we can do it using "Object". I will write a separate post about it later*)

But it can have a method something like **getROproperties**. As of now, QTP is not having such a method.

So, we can read all RO properties from windows registry.

For example, below piece of code can read the name of properties for **"Page"** object from the registry.

Const HKEY_LOCAL_MACHINE = &H80000002

Set oReg = GetObject("winmgmts:{impersonationLevel=impersonate}!\\.\root \default:StdRegProv")

sKeyPath = "SOFTWARE\Mercury Interactive\QuickTest Professional\M icTest\Test Objects\page\Properties"

oReg.EnumValues HKEY_LOCAL_MACHINE, sKeyPath, arrNames

sNames = "List of Properties:" & vbNewLine

For i = 0 to UBound(arrNames)

sNames = sNames & arrNames(i) & vbNewLine

Next

After reading the properties, the script can read each property name from the array "arrNames" and get the run-time object value using GetROproperty method.

You can refer below piece of code.

Set TestPage = Browser("Google").Page("qualitypoint")

For i = 0 to UBound(arrNames)

sNamesRO = sNamesRO & arrNames(i) & ": " & TestPage.GetROPro perty(arrNames(i)) & vbNewLine

Next

MsgBox sNamesRO

Tips for doing effective QTP script Development

1. Read the Requirements **completely** and **repeatedly** till understanding it clearly without any ambiguity. It is better to create **own automation testcase/requirement** based on the manual test cases or business requirement document.
2. Highlight or make note of key requirements in the requirement document. And, highlight the points that are difficult to understand.

3. Don't hesitate to approach the developer/customer/client if you need any clarification in the requirement and also don't hesitate to inform if any of the requirements is unrealistic. Prepare a list of requirements or test cases which can not be automated.

4. QTP Script development Team also should participate in the requirement analysis before starting any application development activity. QTP team can give suggestions (e.g *giving unique name/id for each window so that object identification problem can be avoided when creating QTP scripts*) for the application development Team for improving effectiveness of the QTP script development.

5. Start working on coding/scripting part only after getting clear understanding of the overall Design of the system

6. Enforce Review and Walk Through Activities.

7. Try to setup Development Environment similar to production environment. Otherwise you will face lot of difficulties while running the QTP script against the production application once after completing your script development using development/testing application.

8. Do unit testing immediately after developing each small functionality.

9. Give updates of the progress to the client/customer frequently. If you are facing any difficulty/issue remember to specify in the updates.

10. Make list of things that will vary from Development Environment and Production environment

11. Prepare a user guide document and deliver it along with code.

Some Thoughts on QTP Interview

This Chapter will be useful if you are in a position to start any **Software Testing automation project**.

In this Chapter I am going to write about selecting **appropriate candidate** for your **Team** if you are going to Automate your testing activities using a tool **QTP** (Quick Test Professional). First, we can start with short listing **resumes** of suitable candidates. Basically **QTP** is **just a Tool**. Your Team members can be trained in this Tool easily if they meet **some prerequisites** (e.g knowledge about **Software Testing** Concepts and **programming** fundamental knowledge).

So, it is **not necessary** to short list the candidates with prior work experience with **QTP** unless you want a Team member who needs to start work on QTP script creation from day one of joining your Team.

But, give priority to the knowledge and/or work experience in any kind of Software Testing.

i-e Having hands-on with **manual testing** is a big plus for the Automation tester.

And, you can choose the profiles with knowledge/experience in some other automation test tool also. It will help them learn QTP quickly. Candidates with **vbscript** knowledge/experience can learn QTP fast. **Vbscript** is used in **ASP** (Active server pages). So, you can consider ASP developers also for your **QTP automation Team**.

If you are going to create your **Automation Team** from scratch, at least you should have one resource (Assume **"Team Lead"**) with good experience in QTP. His experience should include creating appropriate **automation framework** and should be expert in handling any **object recognition** issues.

If you are not having such a person to handle any object recognition related issue, it will be difficult to complete the project even if you have good team members to create scripts.

Now, we can discuss about selecting your "Team Lead" and other members.

First we will start with doing interview for your "Team Lead" position in the QTP automation project. (*I mean to say the project which involves automating the functional and regression testing activities using the QTP tool*)

Ask the candidate about handling Object repository.

Ask him to explain any QTP object recognition related challenges he faced during his previous projects. And, ask him to explain how he had solved those issues.

(Anyone who worked in any QTP automation project should have faced such an issue)

Ask the candidate to explain about his understanding about **Automation Framework**.

Ask him how he will deliver the QTP script to production environment from the development environment. In other words, try to get details about his understanding about AOM (Automation Object Model).

Ask him to explain about his understanding about **COM objects** and ask him whether he has handled any COM based application (e.g excel, internet explorer, fso, etc) from QTP script.

Ask him about his approach to split any task to be given to the Team members. His answers should reflect his understanding about proper use of **Shared object repository**.

Ask few questions which can help to reveal his understanding and approach of **Configuration management** in QTP script development environment.

You may ask few questions which can test his thinking about **script maintenance**.

Apart from QTP knowledge, you can ask some questions for

knowing about his basic knowledge in other test automation tools. It will be required for tool evaluation to start any new project. And, it will be useful when doing any migration project.

For example, having some basic knowledge in **winrunner** will be helpful if you are going to convert winrunner scripts into QTP scripts.

Ask him to explain about integrating the QC (Quality Center) with QTP.

Test his knowledge about Database connection with QTP. At least he should be familiar with ADODB, connection string and recordsets. And, he should be familiar with basic SQL queries also.

In case of interviewing Team member, just check his knowledge in Software Testing concepts and knowledge in any programming knowledge. You can ask him about SDLC.

Ask him to explain about **various checkpoints, data driven testing, expert view/keyword view, regular expression** and **recovery scenario** in case he had learnt QTP previously.

Find below the collection of **common interview questions** related to QTP.

It will be useful for the people who are searching job as **Automation test engineer**.

Explain about Object Repository in QTP?
Object Repository is the centralized place for storing the Properties

of objects available in AUT (Application Under Test).

What are the two different Types of Object Repositories available in QTP?

Local Object Repository and Shared Object Repository

What Descriptive Programming and what are the advantages of using Descriptive programming in QTP?

Instead of using Object Repository for storing properties of Test objects, we can straight-away define the properties while writing the script itself using DP. Using Descriptive programming we can start work on writing QTP scripts even before the application under Test is NOT available.

What are the disadvantages of Descriptive Programming in QTP?

The main disadvantage of Descriptive programming is **Maintenance issue**. Since Object repository will be stored in **centralized place**, property definition for any Object can be **easily changed** at any time if the application developer changes the property of the actual object/control. But, in **descriptive programming (DP)** it is **difficult to change** the object property as each QTP developer will be defining object property in many places using DP.

What is framework in QTP?

Framework is nothing but a way or approach of designing the automation scripts. QTP uses various frameworks such as Key Word Driven Testing and Data-driven Testing.

What are the various settings/options available in QTP? And, explain the purpose/scope of them?

Some setting in QTP are specific to Tests and some setting are specific to the IDE.

1. IDE Setting

Settings/options done for QTP IDE will be available only for the particular instance of the QTP installation. i-e If you set an option in QTP installed in Computer1 won't be available in QTP installed in Computer2.. It will be available for all the Tests in Computer1.

2.Test Setting

Settings/options done for particular Test (eg. Test1) will be available for that Test only. It won't be available for other Tests(e.g Test2). But, note that Test1 will keep the settings/options even when we copy the Test1 from Computer1 to Computer2.

The Test setting can be done from **Files->Settings**.

The QTP IDE settings/options can be changed **from Tools->Options.**

How will you set the QTP script to start run at specified time?
We can use **AOM (Automation Object Model)** for creating the vbscript which can be put in windows scheduler for running the QTP script at specified time.

Tell the difference between Action Iteration and Test Iteration in QTP?

Action iterations will be nested within the Test iteration. Action iteration will use the data from local data sheet and the Test Iteration will use the data from Global sheet of the data table.

How will you automate the testing of .NET application which uses thrid-party UI component such as Infragistic netAdvantage?

We should extend capability of **.net add-in** by using **TestAdvantage**

How to handle Passwords in QTP Scripts?
We can encrypt the password using **password encoder** utility provided by QTP. **SetSecure** method can handle this encoded password.

What are the steps/processes involved in QTP automation?
Creating scripts, enhancing scripts, debugging, run script, analyze the results and report the defects.

List some best practices need to be followed while doing QTP automation?
We need to use Shared Object repositories and need to use synchronization point wherever it is required.

What is Object Spy in QTP? And, how to use it?
Object Spy is used for seeing properties and methods of any object in an open application. We can see the properties just by pointing the mouse pointer on the object once after clicking the **hand symbol button** in the **Object Spy** Dialog.

How to use Object Spy if the required object is not visible (i-e window of the object is not active)?

Maximize the window or bring it into the top active window while **holding Ctl key** after clicking the hand symbol button pointer in the Object Spy dialog box. Once the object is visible, release the Ctl key to use the object spy functionality.

How will you read the Test Object property using scripting?
We can use the **"GetTOProperty"** method.

What is the use of *GetTOProperties* method?

This method will be used for getting all the properties and their values of a Test Object.

Which QTP method can be used to get the value of an object property during runtime?
GetROProperty

Will SetTOProperty method make any change in the Object Repository?
No, it won't make any change in the Object Repository. It will just affect the way QTP identifies the object during runtime.

Is it possible to read all the RO properties of a Object?

QTP is not having any built-in method for reading all the RP properties of an Object. But we can write simple script for reading all the properties from **windows registry** and then get the value of each property using the GetROproperty method.

Why we need to automate the software testing using the tools such as QTP?
Automation will avoid human related errors and it can improve the test execution speed also.

Is it possible to automate all the test cases?
No, it is not possible to automate all the test cases. We need to pick the test cases that can be automated.

Tell me about your understanding about QTP?
QTP is a **functional** and **regression** test automation tool. It uses vbscript. It can be easily integrated with **Quality Center** as both are HP products. It supports data driven testing and keyword driven testing. The add-in concept supports various applications such as web, vb, activex, java, TE, and dotNet

Explain QTP Testing process?
QTP Testing involves Creating your test plan, Recording a session on your application, Enhancing your test, Debugging your test, Running your test on a new version of your application, Analyzing the test results and Reporting defects.

QTP trial version installation.

Learning QTP (Quick Test professional) will become easy if we practice some simple tutorials with QTP. HP is providing free trail offer for Quick Test Professional.

Follow below steps to have a QTP set up.

First do keyword search for "quick test professional" in HP website You can see the download link under "trail versions" in the search result.
Once after downloading it you can easily install it just by clicking the setup icon. You will need **maintenance number** while doing installation. You can contact the HP to provide Maintenance number for you.

This Trail version will be valid for **14 days** which is enough to learn QTP.

Wish list for the QTP future release.

We can not say that QTP is a complete Tool even when it has crossed lot of releases. This is due to the fact that Test automation tools are complex to develop.

So, members of a Testing group had a discussion about things that need to be done in coming releases of QTP. I have mentioned below requirement in this discussion.

Allow QTP Script execution while minimizing it so that we need not have separate machine for test script execution.

Find below the requirements collected from others during this discussion. Most of the people want to have the ability for opening multiple tests at a time.

- Provide better support for **Ajax**
- Provide better support for **remote test execution** from Quality Center
- A way to **inherit** test/action resources.
- Better browser support. Support for **non-IE browsers** such as Chrome and Safari
- Need easy **license management**
- A better **coding/IDE environment** with better intellisense, code folding, better debugging (ability to see object contents)..
- Better **version control**. Being able to check out previous versions of a test.
- **Shared code libraries** in QC. i-e ability to save in a common library share that all projects could use.
- Use an **object orientated scripting language** instead of or in addition to VB script
- **Embed the object spy** in the browser similar to firebug for firefox

- Ability to replace object repository with other repositories such as MySql Database
- Reduce the cost. Selenium is evolving and is eating up market share because its free
- Scripts should be able to **run on a locked computer**.
- Add ability to right click on web browser object to spy on it
- Ability to **open more than 1 script at a time**
- User should be able to attach encoded functional library (I.e. .vbe extension file).
- Ability to "pause" a run in order to **edit a script during execution** of multiple iterations
- Support for **FLASH/FLEX** Applications.
- Expose runtime engine as an **API** so we can start using languages other than VBScript.
- Simple and cleaner **uninstall** process
- Improved support for distributed parallel scalable execution (cloud/VM) with reporting concatenation.
- Enhanced function libraries especially **database operations**
- More descriptive error messages **rather than "Generic Error" message.**
- User should be allowed to Export selected portions of Reports
- Ability to see the partial report when the script execution continues

QTP Questions and Answers

Find the answers at the end of the questions.

1) Quick Test Professional (QTP) is used as,
a) Functional Testing tool b) Performance Testing tool c) Usability Testing tool d) Bug tracking tool

2) The below vbscript code is used for,

Set qtApp = CreateObject("QuickTest.Application")
qtApp.Launch

qtApp.Visible = True
a) For launching Function Generator b) For opening QTP using Automation Object Model c) For creating Object Repository from Coding d) For making ActiveScreen visible

---

3) Extension of vbscript function library file is,
a) .vbs b) .mtr c) .lib d) .qtp

---

4) Which one of the below is **External** add-in in QTP?

a) ActiveX add-in b) Visual Basic add-in c) Java add-in d) Web add-in

---

5) Which is used to add report statements in QTP report file?
a) showreport b) reporter.writeline c) reporter.reportEvent d) printReport

---

6) In QTP, properties of Test Objects are stored in
a) ObjectSpy b) Active Screen c) Object Repository d) Library

---

7) Which is used for storing Data used by **Test** Iterations in QTP?
a) Local sheet b) Global Sheet c) Action Sheet d) Object Repository

---

8) Which view will allow us to edit the vbscript code in QTP?
a) Keyword view b) Expert View c) code view d) view source

9) The **Test Management Tool** which can be easily integrated with QTP is,
a) Test Track b) Bugzilla c) Object Repository d) Quality Center

10) Which is used for storing Data used by Action Iteration in QTP?
a) Local sheet b) Global Sheet c) Object Repository d) External Action

11) Outcome of the below QTP code (*vbscript*) is,

```
Set obj = CreateObject("WScript.Shell")
sCmnd = "%windir%\SYSTEM32\rundll32.exe
user32.dll,LockWorkStation"
obj.Run sCmnd, 0, False
```

a) Runtime error b) Computer will be locked automatically. c) Computer will be unlocked d) will throw syntax error

12) Which is used for verifying whether the Actual result matches with expected result in QTP?
a) ObjectSpy b) Object repository c) Checkpoints d) Expert view

13) Which is **built-in** add-in QTP?
a) TE add-in b) java add-in c) web add-in d) .net add-in

14) Setting in one instance of QTP IDE can be transferred to another machine using,
a) Data driver b) Function Generator c) Step Generator d) Automation Object Model

---

Answers

---

(1) a (2) b (3) a (4) c (5) c (6) c (7) b (8) b (9) d (10) a (11) b
(12) c (13) c (14) d

ABOUT THE AUTHOR

Rajamanickam Antonimuthu is Founder and CEO of QualityPoint Technologies, a Software Development Company Established in 2008.

He is interested in writing about Software Development, Web Development, Software Testing, Test Automation, Latest Technology Developments and Motivational Stuff.

www.ingramcontent.com/pod-product-compliance
Lightning Source LLC
Chambersburg PA
CBHW071224050326
40689CB00011B/2441